Presented to

Compassionate Friends

By

Sally Ault

In memory of Bryan Ault

On the Occasion of

Date

Aug 14, 2007

THE
DAWN
OF
HOPE

Encouragement for Those Who Grieve

Eldyn Simons

BARBOUR
PUBLISHING, INC.
Uhrichsville, Ohio

Unless otherwise noted, all Scripture quotations are taken from
the New King James Version. Copyright © 1979, 1980, 1982 by
Thomas Nelson, Inc. Used by permission. All rights reserved.

Scripture quotations marked KJV are taken from the King James
Version of the Bible.

Scripture quotations marked TLB are taken from The Living
Bible, copyright © 1971. Used by permission of Tyndale House
Publishers, Inc., Wheaton, Illinois, 60189. All rights reserved.

Published by Barbour Publishing, Inc., P. O. Box 719,
Uhrichsville, Ohio 44683 http://www.barbourbooks.com

Member of the
Evangelical Christian
Publishers Association

Printed in the United States of America.

DEDICATION

In memory of Philip. . .
and with appreciation for all who love me.

CONTENTS

Editor's Foreword 11

Introduction
The Dawn of Comfort 15

Part I: The Death of a Son
 1. Safety in the Midst of Death 19
 2. The Fellowship of His Suffering 22
 3. A Community of Pain 25
 4. O My Son! 29
 5. The Song of Hope 33
 6. Comforters 36
 7. Healing Through Sharing 40
 8. Tearstained Praise 43
 9. Times Like These 46
10. Life Goes On 49
11. Acquainted with Grief 52
12. The Long Journey Toward Healing . . . 55
13. A Solid Bond 60
14. Songs of Deliverance 63
15. A Common Language 66
16. The Rainbow of Hope 69

Part II: Good-Byes

1. Saying Good-Bye to a Spouse 75
2. Losing the Older Generation 78
3. Empty Hearts and Empty Arms. 82
4. Safe in Jesus' Arms. 86
5. Saying Good-Bye to Our Hopes 89
6. A God Who Understands 93
7. Pools of Blessing 96
8. A Simple Prayer. 105
9. Why?. 109
10. No Shortcuts 112

Part III: God of All Comfort

1. Thirsting for Comfort 117
2. Trust: The Beginning of Comfort. . . . 121
3. God's Touch. 125
4. Hope in the Darkness 128
5. A Bulwark of Love. 131
6. Our Security Blanket 134
7. The Comfort of Memory 138
8. Comfort for Every Grief 142
9. A Loving Presence 145
10. Comfort Shared. 148
11. Conduits for God's Peace 151
12. Dare to Love 155
13. A Sweet Aroma 158
14. Simple Acts of Love. 161

Part IV: Victory in the Midst of Affliction
  1. We Are Loved 167
  2. The Fiery Furnace of Affliction 170
  3. Light in the Lion's Den 174
  4. Candles in the Darkness. 177
  5. Keeping the Faith 181
  6. The Faith of Job. 185
  7. Hope 189

Part V: The Shepherd's Psalm
  1. The Person of the Shepherd. 195
  2. The Provision of the Shepherd. 198
  3. The Protection of the Shepherd 202
  4. The Preparation of the Shepherd 206
  5. The Promise of the Shepherd. 209

Part VI: The Light of Dawn
  1. Joy in the Morning. 215
  2. Lime Lake, 1938 218
  3. The Promise of the Dawn 221
  4. Homecoming. 225

Part VII: Finding Comfort in the Scriptures

Editor's Foreword

I edit all sorts of books by all sorts of people. I am often inspired by the words with which I work, and I gain new insights from their authors' thoughts.

But editing this book was a new experience for me, because I lived with the author through the experiences he describes in this book. The sorrows of which he writes touched my own heart. You see, the author is my father.

I suppose most of us take our parents for granted to some extent, especially when we are teenagers. But as I worked on this book, I was humbled by something I had never thought much about before: my father's integrity. In this book—and in his life—he dares to be honest about his own pain and anguish. And all the while his faith in God's undying, joyful love is never fazed.

In my own life, I have sometimes been confused by the idea that a true Christian, a Christian with real faith, should never be overwhelmed with anguish or despair or anger. I have mistaken faith for happiness, and I feared that if I was swept with negative emotions, then I had somehow misplaced my faith. From this perspective, our dark feelings become our enemies, something to be fought and denied.

But as I read *The Dawn of Hope,* I realized that my father's faith has been his companion *through* his times of desperate pain and dreary depression. He has always had the courage to walk through the dark emotions—and his faith has walked with him, undaunted.

The week after I finished my work on this book, my father was diagnosed with pancreatic cancer. We did not think we would have him with us much longer, and the weeks that followed were terrifying and dark. But I carried with me the promise I had learned from this book and from my father's life: Death cannot conquer love. Through Christ, we will never really lose the people we love so much.

Throughout his writing, my father speaks of "the dawn." When he uses the lowercase, he is usually referring to the moment when comfort at last sheds its light on our despair. And when he speaks of Dawn, with a capital D, he is talking about the morning when Eternity's sun rises, the moment when we at last see Christ face-to-face.

This year, dawn broke for our family when my father's doctor told us some wonderful news: The tumor was benign and my father would recover. We would get to keep him a while longer.

But I am glad that no matter what the future holds, no matter how many times death asks us to say good-bye, no matter how dark and long the nights ahead, the gospel tells us that the Dawn of Eternity will come. The promise of that glorious sunrise is the comfort this book offers to all who mourn.

This book is a true story. I know it is true, because I witnessed it. And I am grateful to my father for writing down the truth of his life.

Ellyn Sanna, editor

INTRODUCTION
The Dawn of Comfort

That night was so very long. Beside me, my wife had finally succumbed to a troubled sleep, but hour after hour, I lay sleepless, my heart broken. All was dark within me. My parents used to insist that boys don't cry, and I'd believed them all my life; but now the fountains of my soul opened as I wept for my only son, dead on a Peruvian mountainside.

Even the darkest nights end, though. Slowly the dawn did come—and as the first light shone through our bedroom window, I heard the morning music of a song sparrow. It was God's song sparrow, for its notes carried a message to my heart: "His eye is on the sparrow and I know He cares for me."

At that moment, God began His healing comfort in my heart. And in many ways, in many places, and through many people, God continues to give comfort.

If you have never had your heart broken, if you have never felt all alone, if you have not known the darkness, the utter soul-wrenching darkness of grief, then maybe this book is not for you—but I believe it is. All of us, one way or another, sooner or later, experience the long, dark night of grief. But this book is also about a Heavenly Father who cares so much when life hurts that He does something about it. And it is about our being equipped to comfort others. Most of all it is about the light of that wonderful Dawn that will one day end the darkness of even our most painful nights. Christ has promised to put an end to death and sorrow. When that wonderful morning dawns, what a day it will be!

As you read this book, my prayer for you is one that the apostle Paul prayed for the church at Thessalonica:

Now may our Lord Jesus Christ Himself, and our God and Father, who has loved us and given us everlasting consolation and good hope by grace, comfort your hearts and establish you in every good word and work.
2 THESSALONIANS 2:16–17

PART I

THE DEATH OF A SON

In this book's first part, I want to tell you about my own intimate acquaintance with grief: the death of my son, Philip Eldyn Simons, when he was not quite seventeen. As I share my story with you, I hope you will find comfort and hope as you face your own sorrows.

As a pastor, I often dealt with the grief of others. But I suppose I took my own blessings for granted. In those days, I was not intimately acquainted with grief.

One August, all that changed. . . .

1

SAFETY IN THE MIDST OF DEATH

The LORD shall preserve you from all evil;
He shall preserve your soul.
The LORD shall preserve
your going out and your coming in
From this time forth,
and even forevermore.
PSALM 121:7–8

By some standards, Bethy and I had a large family, but we considered our family of four girls and one boy just right. Each was special in his or her own right. It was and is a great family, full of fun and love.

In 1970, Philip—our fourth child—was sixteen and a junior in high school. He asked us if he could participate in a summer exchange student program to South America, preferably Peru, to see and experience that land of mystery and ancient civilizations. We made arrangements with International Fellowship of Buffalo, New York, for Philip to go to Peru. The Fellowship chartered a plane and on June 19, 1970, young people began arriving at New York's Kennedy International Airport.

We took Philip to Buffalo that day to catch his flight to Kennedy. The flight was delayed, but finally, with a wave of his hand, we saw our son for the last time as he boarded the plane. Trusting the promises of Psalm 121:7–8, we believed that God would keep him safe from evil and preserve both his going out and his coming in.

But when tragedies strike, it's hard to believe the psalm's promises. All of us dread the clouds of sorrow and loss that move across our lives' sunshine, throwing darkness and gloom across our hearts. But though we do not realize it, those very clouds are full of God's mercy. Out of our heartsick pain, He will rain His blessings on our lives. And He will not only preserve our loved ones' souls; He will preserve ours as well.

COMFORT FOR THOSE WHO GRIEVE

Ye fearful saints, fresh courage take,
The clouds ye so much dread
Are big with mercy, and shall break
In blessings on your head.
— WILLIAM COWPER

Lord, we put our lives into Your hands. We trust You
to preserve us from all evil, even in the face of death.

2

THE FELLOWSHIP OF
HIS SUFFERING

*That I may know Him
and the power of His resurrection,
and the fellowship of His sufferings,
being conformed to His death, if, by any means,
I may attain to the resurrection from the dead.*
PHILIPPIANS 3:10–11

August 9, 1970 was a beautiful Sunday. My wife and I were pastoring a small country church at the time, and God was blessing us there. We felt God's presence in the services, and the church was growing and deepening. On that Sunday morning, I brought the last of three sermons from the third chapter of Philippians, that portion of the letter where Paul speaks of a complete yielding to Christ, so that Christ and His resurrection life might be truly ours.

As I spoke that Sunday on "The Fellowship of His Suffering," I had no concept of the depth of real suffering and pain we were to face that very day. How very easy it is to speak! But how hard to actually face and experience the awful anguish of the soul that comes through the hand of God, even though we know that it is the hand of His love.

That afternoon was a quiet, restful time. After church, we spent a short time visiting with my wife's family, and then we had the evening service back at church. We went to bed early and were soon fast asleep. All of our girls were home except for our daughter Judy, who was married and living in Virginia. And so we peacefully slept!

That same afternoon in Peru, Lansa flight 502 lifted off from the mountain airport of Cuzco for its flight to Lima on the coast. Among the 102 passengers and crew were 49 American exchange students who were bringing to a close four wonderful days in the Inca capital in the high Andes. There in the ancient land of the Incas, they had explored Machu Picchu, Tambomachay and its fountains of water, and Cuzco. They went to the markets and found gifts for their loved ones back home, silver and gold jewelry wrought in exquisite designs, ponchos, and alpaca sweaters.

None of the students knew what lay ahead, any more than those of us at home knew that soon we would be experiencing the fellowship of Christ's suffering.

I'll hold thy hand when the storm clouds
*   gather,*
I'll hold thy hand when the thunders
*   roar.*
When the deluge breaks in all its fury,
I'll hold thy hand till the storm is o'er.
               MRS. M. J. CHRISTIE

We do not know the future, Lord—but You do. Even when hard times come, keep us close to You.

3

A COMMUNITY
OF PAIN

Weep with those who weep.
ROMANS 12:15

On that August Sunday afternoon, the plane, airborne and gaining altitude, suddenly lost one engine. The pass and 20,000-foot mountains lay ahead. Fearing the pass, the pilot informed the tower at Cuzco that he was returning to the airport. He was ordered to continue his flight to Lima on three engines.

Flight 502 was a poorly maintained plane. Earlier that day it had flown from Lima over the Andes to Iquitos in the jungles of eastern Peru. On takeoff from Iquitos, the motor had quit time after time. Finally, still running erratically, the plane made its flight to Lima. Unrepaired, it flew from there to Cuzco. A businessman on the plane reported later how relieved he had been when the plane landed.

Now, the pilot disobeyed his orders to continue on to Lima. He swung wide to make his descent to the airport. There on the mountainside above a little village called San Jeronimo, the plane struck the mountain; a few minutes after 3:00 P.M. the plane exploded in a ball of fire. Everyone died except the copilot.

In our sorrow and loss, we said, "If only that pilot had obeyed orders. If only he had trusted those other three motors." There are always so many "if only's." But he did disobey. The plane did crash. One hundred and one did die. According to the copilot, the pilot died with a prayer on his lips: "God have mercy on our souls." So many lives, so many promising young people and their futures, so many left behind devastated with sudden sorrow.

A board of investigation found that the cause of the accident was ten percent mechanical and ninety percent pilot error. For all of us who lost our children and loved ones that report was little comfort. Our precious ones were gone from us.

And so while we enjoyed a quiet, restful

Sunday afternoon, the plane burned with intense heat. Our son was one of a few who, when the tail broke off, was thrown out and did not burn in the flames. With a strange relief, we heard this news from his Peruvian host father, Alfonso Leon Prado, who identified his body.

Those were hard days in America and in Peru, days of darkness, despair, emptiness, and helplessness. Nearly five thousand miles separated us. We could only wait and imagine, hoping that soon Philip's body would be returned to us.

Today, every time I hear of another plane down, I pray. My heart goes out to those who wait for news, for I know their pain. We share a fellowship of suffering; we are a community of pain. And Christ is also a part of this sorrowing community. He, too, mourns our losses. And sometime, somewhere, in the light of that wonderful Dawn, He will restore to us all that we have lost.

Faith cannot be unanswered;
Her feet are firmly planted on the rock;
Amid the wildest storms she stands
undaunted.
Nor quails before the loudest thunder
shock,

*She knows Omnipotence hath heard her
    prayer,
And cries, "It shall be done, sometime,
    somewhere."*
            —MRS. OPHELIA G. ADAMS

*Lord, we don't understand why tragedies strike so
often. But we pray today for all those around the
world who are hurting. We plant our feet on faith's
rock and wait for the Dawn.*

4

O MY SON!

Then the king was deeply moved,
and went up to the chamber
over the gate, and wept.
And as he went, he said thus:
"O my son Absalom—
my son, my son Absalom—
if only I had died in your place!
O Absalom my son, my son!"
2 SAMUEL 18:33

We went to bed early that Sunday night and were soon sleeping deeply. Awakened by the telephone at about 10:45 P.M., I answered sleepily, wondering who could be calling at that hour. It was Neal, my son-in-law in Virginia. He had just heard a news report that a plane was down at Cuzco,

Peru, with American exchange students on board. I quickly turned the TV on for the 11:00 news, and the news announcer verified Neal's message. All on the plane were believed dead except for the copilot (who had been thrown from the cockpit into a grove of eucalyptus trees). The students in the news report had the same schedule as Philip's tour. Flying to Cuzco on Thursday, they had visited the ancient Inca capital and its environs and were now returning to their host families in the Lima area. An awful certainty settled upon us: Philip, our son, was dead.

I tried to deny the awful fact, but I could not. Reluctantly I went to our daughters' bedrooms and awakened them to the shocking news that we were sure their brother was dead. It was a somber gathering there in the living room. It seemed so impossible.

I phoned the exchange organization. "Yes, the plane is down." They were waiting for word from the state department listing the dead before notifying the parents. About 12:30 A.M. they phoned. Philip was one of those killed. Our only son, our mischievous, handsome, gifted son and brother, was not coming home to tell his tales of Peru. He was not coming home!

I now knew the agony of David weeping for his son Absalom. That night my heart broke and

I wept as I had never wept before. And then I began to appreciate the words of my sermon's text: "the fellowship of His suffering." Our Heavenly Father was so very close! We cried. We called on the Father in prayer. We knew He cared. And we knew our Lord Jesus Christ understood, for wasn't He "a Man of sorrows and acquainted with grief"?

We had often sung the words of this song, but now they sang to us:

Does Jesus care when my heart is pained
Too deeply for mirth and song;
As the burdens press and the cares distress,
And the way grows weary and long?

O yes, He cares; I know He cares,
His heart is touched with my grief;
When the days are weary, the long nights
*   dreary.*
I know my Savior cares.

Does Jesus care when my way is dark
With a nameless dread and fear?
As the daylight fades into deep night
*   shades,*
Does He care enough to be near?

The Dawn of Hope

Does Jesus care when I've said good-bye
To the dearest on earth to me,
And my sad heart aches till it nearly
      breaks—
Is it aught to Him? Does He care?

O yes, He cares; I know He cares.
His heart is touched with my grief;
When the days are weary, the long nights
      dreary,
I know my Savior cares.
                    —FRANK E. GRAEFF, 1901

Thank You, Lord, that when our hearts break, You
care for us.

5

THE SONG OF HOPE

In Him was life, and the life was the light of men.
And the light shines in the darkness,
and the darkness did not comprehend it.
JOHN 1:4–5

That dark night when we knew our son was dead, my wife picked up her Bible, and it fell open to the beatitudes in Matthew 5. As though underlined by the very finger of God's love, she saw only these words: "Blessed are those who mourn, for they shall be comforted." Already our Father was bringing a few streaks of dawn's hope into the dark night of our despair.

And He was always there during this time, lavishing His love upon us. But even then there were times we hurt so much we did not grasp that comfort and love were available.

I welcomed dawn's bright sky after that long sleepless night. That was when God sent the song sparrow to remind us again that He was still in control. "Are not two sparrows sold for a copper coin? And not one of them falls to the ground apart from your Father's will. . . . Do not fear therefore; you are of more value than many sparrows" (Matthew 10:29, 31). In the darkness of my loss, in the darkness of that long, long night, my soul hungered for something, some light. Philip was dead. God, knowing my need, so wonderfully sent His messenger of hope: The song sparrow sang and a new day dawned.

And I learned that God is not asleep while we sorrow. He is in the darkness of the darkest nights. A new dawn, a new day, is ahead. It is ours by trust and faith in His compassionate love.

> *"The souls of men are never dead."*
> *The songs of bird seem not to die—*
> *Their echoes sound throughout the sky—*
> *It's earthly life that ends, we know;*
> *A soul, like song, leaves an afterglow.*
> —RUTH ALLA WAGER

Thank You, Lord, that You are here with us in the midst of our pain. We know that all earthly life must come to an end. But help us to hear hope singing softly through the darkness.

6

COMFORTERS

Share with me in the sufferings for the gospel
according to the power of God,
who has saved us and called us
with a holy calling.
2 TIMOTHY 1:8–9

As we awoke reluctantly to our new day and its
ever-present sorrow, we drew together to deal
with whatever came next, to do whatever had to
be done to face a future that contained no Philip.
There was no way to change what had happened:
We had to accept our loss and get through it
somehow.

I once saw a cartoon that in a way depicted
our dilemma. The cartoon portrayed a maternity
admissions desk, a long-suffering receptionist, a
very pregnant wife, and a worried and disturbed

husband. The caption was simple: "Are you sure, dear, that you want to go through with this?" There are times when the only way is to go straight ahead. There are no other real alternatives. Birth is one of those times—and so is death. We cannot escape death's reality. It must be faced and accepted before it can be conquered.

But God helps—and He sends other helpers. The news of the accident spread through the community and among our family and friends. The radio and television were filled with reports of the crash and the loss of five of the students who lived in the Rochester, New York, area. The phone began to ring. Friends called in their support.

Most of our friends came with one purpose in mind: to put their arms of love around us and join their hearts with ours as we wept for Philip. And so very many came during those awful days of waiting. Many others phoned; many more sent cards and letters. How we needed them all! We needed to know we were not alone in our grief. Food came in with them—casseroles, bread, cakes. But besides these tangible gifts, besides these people's presence, they also all brought the special unique gifts of their hearts, for each person was part of a divine program for healing—a fragrance from the Lord, a precious memorial poured out upon us in love.

We soon realized that this was not our grief alone. The whole community and our church family shared our grief for the boy they had come to love. As they sorrowed with us, they brought us a measure of comfort.

Our extended family laid down their cares and supported us in ours. Many came with reluctance and dread, not knowing what to do or say. But they came.

The loss of a loved one makes us feel frightened and alone—but love can build a hedge around our hearts, a shelter of continuing strength. If you are hurting today, allow others to give you that shelter of comfort—and then reach out yourself to help build a hedge of love around another's heart.

Together we'll share it,
Together we'll bear it,
Together we'll see it through.

Alone I was weary,
Alone it was heavy
Till I rested the weight upon you.
—RUTH ALLA WAGER

*Build the hedge of Your love around our hearts, Lord.
Be our Shelter in the midst of pain. Send Your people to speak Your love and lighten our heavy loads of
sorrow.*

7

HEALING THROUGH SHARING

*Now all who believed were together,
and had all things in common.*
ACTS 2:44

Philip's body did not come home until nine days after his death, and the funeral was held August 19. Those ten days were nearly unbearable as we dealt with his death from such an enormous geographical distance. We felt so helpless. My wife had just had surgery, and grief brought on complications.

Yet in spite of all the difficulties and grief, I find myself thinking more of the good things that happened during that period: the manifestations of love and concern so lavishly poured out upon us by so many. I have heard that elephants gather to protect the weak and injured, and during those days of grief, I felt as if everyone circled around us to protect us from further hurt and harm.

Several came to stay with us who were of great help. Our house was large and we adjusted easily to the extra guests and willing hands. What I remember most about them was the out-poured love and support; they knew our need and they were there. God in His infinite knowledge and love sent them. Cards, letters, and phone calls poured in. Best of all, we were conscious of the prayers raised in intercession for us, not only by those close to us, but even by strangers.

During that time, we experienced one highlight of love we didn't expect. Nine of Philip's senior class friends came to see us. They were having a difficult time with Philip's death and it was hard for them to come, but they did. We talked, we laughed, and we cried together as we remembered Philip. We were one in our sorrow. We heard things about our boy we had never known: his kindness to all, his understanding, his strength of character, his wise counsels, and most of all, his Christian wit-ness. We had much to laugh about and much to cry for. Above all, those young people made us feel proud. They left, but the joy of their com-ing lingers on. God continued His healing.

If you are hurting today, you may feel as though all comfort is completely beyond your sight. But wait and see. God will surprise you. He will send a little bit of heaven's light to you, maybe through someone you least expect. Your job is to simply wait upon the Lord—and then pass on whatever light you receive to someone else who walks in darkness.

You cannot "go to heaven,"
For heaven goes with you;
It isn't some place far away
Beyond the spacious blue.

Heaven dwells within a heart,
Within a soul and mind;
We take that heaven with us
When we love and serve mankind.
       —ANONYMOUS

Lord, thank You that when we share our love with each other, we catch a glimpse of heaven's light.

8

TEARSTAINED PRAISE

Why are you cast down, O my soul?
And why are you disquieted within me?
Hope in God; for I shall yet praise Him,
The help of my countenance and my God.
PSALM 42:11

The Saturday evening after Philip's death we finally received direct word from Peru—a phone call from his Peruvian family, the Leon-Prados. The connection was poor and noisy. One of the sons, Jorge, spoke English with a strong accent. I could just catch the words that Philip's body was being released and would be flown home the next day. We were grateful for that phone call and those who made it. In the early hours of Tuesday morning, Philip finally came home to the local funeral parlor.

I remember well much about the funeral service, but I cannot remember the funeral message nor can I recall the words of comfort. I only know we *were* comforted and for many it was a time of closure. I believe songs have a part in our saying "good-bye." Rev. Alton Shea, brother of George Beverly Shea, sang, "In the Sweet By and By," and "In Times Like These." This last song was to become a special bulwark for me when grief threatened to overcome me. For months I sang the words. I whistled the tune. I carried it in my heart.

Over a mile-long funeral cortege wound its way the five miles to where we buried our son in the cemetery overlooking his beloved hills, the site of so many of his walks. We closed the committal service with the "Doxology," praising God for the gift of Philip's life.

On his grave we placed a gray marble gravestone that was etched with the picture of rugged Andean mountains, a rising sun, and these words: "He saw a new sunrise in the Andes." At the bottom are carved the words from Malachi 4:2, "But to you who fear My name the Sun of Righteousness shall arise with healing in His wings." And there above all is his name: Philip Eldyn Simons, September 9, 1953–August 9, 1970.

How short was his life and yet how full he filled that life with the joy and excitement of living! We praise God for him.

Even death cannot erase the joy and love God gives to us through each other. It's hard to sing a song of praise when the night seems so very dark. But one day the Sun of Righteousness will arise, with healing in His wings—and then we will see Philip again.

> *I cannot say, and I will not say*
> *That he is dead. He is just away.*
> *With a cheery smile, and a wave of the*
>   *hand,*
> *He has wandered into an unknown*
>   *land. . . .*
> *Think of him still as the same. I say,*
> *He is not dead—he is just away.*
>   —JAMES WHITCOMB RILEY

Lord, thank You for Your comfort. We praise You through our tears, knowing that one day we will see our loved ones again.

9

TIMES LIKE THESE

He only is my rock and my salvation;
He is my defense;
I shall not be moved.
PSALM 62:6

The days following Philip's funeral were difficult as we tried to adjust to the fact that our boy was dead. We would not see him again in this life. That fact was nearly impossible for us to comprehend.

Then tragedy struck again. Bethy's father, eighty-two years old but still actively farming, was injured in an accident. As he worked on a hillside behind a small tractor, the tractor came out of gear. It knocked him down, dragged him several feet, and then one of the rear wheels ran over him, crushing his ribs and pelvis. He was dying when he arrived at the hospital.

This seemed like far more than we could bear. Sometimes life seems to pile up on us sorrow upon sorrow, just as it did with Job, who suffered loss after loss. In times like these, we need to anchor our life in God. He is the only Rock who will hold firm and solid, no matter how wild the storms of life.

We turned to God in prayer for Dad's life—and God intervened. Dad's heart was strong, and in spite of his severe injuries, he finally recovered his health. His bones healed, and he lived for ten more years. God knew how much we could stand, and He knew we could not bear losing Dad and our son all at once. Dad's farming days were over, but by late fall, he was walking in a twisted way, helping Mother around the house.

God continued His faithfulness in bringing more healing to our hearts and minds. We knew we could rely on Him for strength as the days went by. Job's wife advised him to curse God and die, and when we suffer loss, bitterness is always a temptation. But in the time after Philip's death, we knew God had not abandoned us. Like Job, we trusted in His love.

The Dawn of Hope

In times like these you need a Savior,
In times like these you need an anchor.
Be very sure, be very sure
Your anchor holds and grips the Solid Rock.
                    —RUTH CAYE JONES

Lord, we thank You for the anchor of Your love. No matter what happens, help us to never lose our grip on You, our Solid Rock.

10

LIFE GOES ON

But thanks be to God,
who gives us the victory
through our Lord Jesus Christ.
1 CORINTHIANS 15:57

We missed Philip with an inexpressible ache deep in our very beings. But God heard our prayers and gave us the continuing assurance of His presence and concern. During this time, I kept up my duties as a pastor with an even greater sense of my responsibilities. The coming of the new school year brought the added responsibility of our teaching jobs, my wife as a fourth-grade teacher and me as a high school art teacher.

I approached my teaching with mixed feelings. On the one hand, it was a way to keep my mind occupied—but I dreaded the fact that so many of Philip's close friends were taking art just to be near me in their grief. I was afraid that seeing their faces every day would only bring home to me again and again the one face that was missing.

I have never taught a more wonderful group, however. So often that semester sudden anguish would come upon me and I would flee to the corridor. The students understood and stood with me. I have always thanked God for these young people who, by giving their love, brought more healing to my heart.

But our hard times were not over. After a few weeks of teaching, I became seriously ill with pneumonia and missed six weeks of school. Then Shirley, a student of mine and the daughter of a good friend, was killed in a car accident. Once more God comforted us together, teachers, students, and her parents.

And then came Christmas. Everyone who has lost a loved one knows the sadness of holidays. That Christmas proved no exception. I remember well the awful feeling of hope that out of the crowd of shoppers our son would come to ask our advice or to show us a gift. But he never came. We had no heart for shopping or festivities or family gatherings. In times like this, it is good to have other children. They expect Christmas and so you proceed. Somehow the holidays became somewhat normal.

Remember, though, no rule says you must be happy and festive at Christmas. The real meaning of Christmas is not about colored lights and decorations, bells and presents. No, the true meaning of Christmas is this: Jesus loved us so much that He was born in the midst of our dark, sorrowing world. His coming does not depend on festivities and laughter and singing. He can be born in your life just as it is, with all its darkness and pain.

> I'll hold thy hand then—child, take
>   courage,
>   For thou art always in My care.
> My hand shall lead thee on triumphant
>   Through pearly gates to that land so
>   fair.
>   —MRS. M. J. CHRISTIE

It is so hard to go on with life, Lord, knowing that our loved one will not be with us. But we'll take Your hand, Lord. Please give us the victory over our lives' dark sorrows.

11

ACQUAINTED WITH GRIEF

He is despised and rejected by men,
A Man of sorrows and acquainted with grief.
ISAIAH 53:3

Our Heavenly Father has sent us many wonderful friends and acquaintances. One of the great treasures of our lives has been their friendship, understanding, love, and especially their prayers. Through them our lives have been enriched and deepened beyond measure. We shall ever remain in their debt for being there when we have needed them most.

I appreciate my friends and acquaintances—but I can't say that I have appreciated my acquaintance with grief. Yet I must admit that often through its acquaintance I gained a special sense of God's purpose and love.

As a pastor, I had always shared the grief of my parishioners—and how great was the grief when loved ones and friends slipped from our lives! Always the grief was real and very deep. But when the greatest grief of my life struck unexpectedly and devastatingly, I really learned the agony of the soul.

When Philip was a small boy, a couple in our church gave the clothes of their son to us for Philip's use. Their son had died from complications after a simple tonsillectomy. At the time, we didn't fully appreciate their sorrow and grief. We expressed our appreciation for the clothes, but only after our own son's death several years later could I go to that father and say, "Now I understand." Together we grieved for our sons. We were both acquainted with grief.

Jesus was no stranger to grief either. He experienced human sorrow—and when we hurt, He understands. He is there with us in the pain. Like us, He is acquainted with grief.

> 'Tis the human touch in this world that
>   counts,
>   The touch of your hand and mine
>   Which means far more to the fainting heart
>   Than shelter and bread and wine;

The Dawn of Hope

For shelter is gone when the night is o'er,
And bread lasts only a day,
But the touch of the hand and the sound of
the voice
Sing on in the soul alway.
—Spencer Michael Free

Thank You, Lord, that You understand our grief.
Help us to share Your love and understanding with
others who are sorrowing.

12

THE LONG JOURNEY
TOWARD HEALING

If I take the wings of the morning,
And dwell in the uttermost parts of the sea,
Even there Your hand shall lead me,
And Your right hand shall hold me.
PSALM 139:9–10

As a boy, I spent many Sunday afternoons under the pines on the top of our hill. I listened to the soft voice of the wind through the pine needles and contemplated impossible but glorious trips and adventures. I was a farm boy, but the acres of the farm did not set the bounds of my vision. Although this was the time of the Great Depression, the 1930s, that farm in western New York

State was a place of dreams of far-off places and great exploits. The times were filled with despair, but on my hilltop I saw only impossible—but glorious—journeys. I envisioned shipping out on a freighter to see the oceans and the ports and the peoples of the great world I had read so much about.

As it turned out, my one and only trip on a freighter wasn't around the world. In July of 1972, two years after Philip's death, my wife Bethy, our fourteen-year-old daughter Ellyn (our youngest), and I boarded a freighter, the *Santa Barbara*, for a voyage of fourteen days to Callao, Peru. Despite the circumstances, that trip proved to be beyond all my boyhood expectations. It was truly a dream come true.

We had wondered about Philip's life so far away in Peru, and we wanted to meet his host family with whom we continued to correspond. We wanted to see the sights he had seen and feel what he had felt. So it was that our trip to Peru became necessary in our thinking. Since Philip had died in a plane crash, my wife was reluctant to fly, and we went down by freighter.

We sailed from Port Newark into the soft summer twilight and watched the skyscrapers of New York City disappear into the darkness. Our adventure had begun! Each day of our voyage brought new wonders. We explored foreign ports and on our days at sea we watched flying fish glide below us on silvery, gossamer wings. Dolphins rolled and played about us, and one day we saw the huge, dark shape of Galapagos turtles swimming beside us, their serpentine necks stretched out above the water. At night the sky was ablaze with stars and constellations I had never seen before.

We hated to leave behind our enchanted time on the ship, but all too soon we reached the port of Callao. There, we finally looked down into the faces of the family we had come so far to see—the Leon-Prados of Chosica.

I know they were disappointed that we knew so little Spanish. We were disappointed that they knew so little English. But love and patience and our trusty *diccionario* soon made us comfortable with each other. These were the ones who had cared for Philip in their home, with whom he had spoken last. They grieved for our boy also. Their love for us was obvious, and it still is after all these years.

In their home in Chosica, the sun always shone in a cloudless sky. Here in this sunlit place, we began to picture Philip's last days. We had come looking for comfort. And God did not disappoint us.

How strange that God brought this journey of wonder and discovery after my darkest night. On that August night two years before, I would never have believed I would be capable of feeling joy ever again. And yet God knew His plans for me, and as I trusted Him, He brought healing to my heart.

He will do the same for each one of you. Right now you may be in the midst of night so dark that you doubt the dawn will ever come. But be patient. Your own long journey to comfort and healing may not take you across the equator or to a foreign country. But in one way or another, I am quite sure that it will take you to many unexpected places, places of which you may never have even dreamed.

Of course none of us would choose to make this long journey if we had the choice. But we can be confident that no matter how long our voyage may be, God will continue to lead us. Even in "the uttermost parts of the sea," His hand will grip ours. He will travel with us, teaching us how to bear the pain, how to laugh again, how to once more taste life's sweetness. He will never leave us.

Teach me how to laugh, dear God,
  When my laughter's gone;
Teach me how to bear the pain
  And still keep fighting on;
Teach me how to share Thy love
  In what I do and say,
So all I meet will find life sweet
  For having shared my day.
                    —RUTH ALLA WAGER

We don't always know where we're going, Lord. We can't see our destination. But we trust You to always lead us.

13

A Solid Bond

Holding fast to the Head,
from whom all the body,
nourished and knit together
by joints and ligaments,
grows with the increase that is from God.
COLOSSIANS 2:19

We arrived in Peru on Sunday, July 30. The following Friday we took the long bus ride to Arequipa in the south and then went by train up the Andes to Juliaca near Lake Titicaca. We then took another train up the great valley between the Andes ranges to Cuzco, arriving on Monday. It was a trip of nearly twelve hundred miles.

To walk the streets of Cuzco is to step back in time. First you are conscious of the colonial

Spanish buildings: the public buildings and cathedrals. But as you look more closely, you become aware that this city is far older than the red-tiled city of stone and adobe that the Spaniards built. The old Inca walls are everywhere, foundations for the newer buildings.

The Incan Temple of the Sun was not far from the hotel where we stayed in Cuzco. The temple's beautiful walls—and the Inca walls everywhere—stand as a tribute to those skilled stone masons who formed them. Many great Spanish buildings have been built upon them and beside them. The great earthquakes of the Andes have often crushed the intruders. But the Inca walls still stand, formed of great interlocking, many-angled blocks of granite, so tightly fitted that a knife blade cannot be inserted between them. No one knows how such hard stone could have been carved with such precision. The people had no iron, no wheels, and no written language, yet theirs was a culture equal to any of the great civilizations of the world. And these stones testify to their past glory.

In our times of grief, we can learn a lesson from these interlocking megaliths. The secret of victory over our adversities is to have lives so well formulated, so well integrated, so joined in all their parts, that nothing can shake our faith in the unconditional love of our Savior. In Colossians 2:19 Paul spoke of our bodies' healthy union as a metaphor for the solid bond of our relationship to the Father. Our responsibility is to hold fast to God, to snuggle close so nothing can come between us. His part is to cover us with His love, to encourage and nourish us with His life that we may be fruitful in our service to Him, no matter what conditions surround us.

God loveth thee—then be content;
Whate'er thou hast, His love hath sent;
Come pain or pleasure, good or ill,
His love is round about thee still.
Then murmur not, nor anxious be,
Rest thou in peace, God loveth thee!

God loveth thee. Though dark the night,
His smile shall make thy pathway bright,
When weary ways before thee lie,
The Lord, thy Helper, draweth nigh.
Press bravely on, the end to see:
Be not dismayed, God loveth thee.
                                        —ANONYMOUS

Thank You, Lord, for loving us. Help us to stay close to You.

14

SONGS OF DELIVERANCE

You are my hiding place;
You shall preserve me from trouble;
You shall surround me with songs of deliverance.
PSALM 32:7

Cuzco was not only culturally and historical fascinating; it was also the place where our son died. The Tuesday that we were there was the second anniversary of the accident, August 9, 1972. A memorial mass and service was planned at the crash site on the mountainside.

That morning no one else came for a long time, and we had the mountainside to ourselves. We had the chance to make our peace with that place of death and destruction. And God did give peace in that awful place where Philip died.

The earth was still scorched, littered with the small rubble of burnt cloth, combs, and scraps of duralumin. But despite that, the air was quiet and tranquil up there on the mountainside. God was very close, and He spoke a special peace to our hearts. That time of waiting was one of great healing. I don't know why or how, but somehow God gave us peace and comfort as we stood and contemplated this place where Philip had died.

The mountains rose far above us, reaching up to jagged peaks against the intense blue Andean sky. Below us was the broad terraced valley with its fields, eucalyptus trees, and humble villages of adobe. A wisp of smoke drifted up from a cooking fire. Cattle grazed peacefully. Tiny figures worked in the fields. The village of San Jeronimo lay just below us with its narrow unpaved streets and adobe walls. Off to the right about two or three miles were the runways of the airport. Beyond, red-tiled Cuzco lay glowing in the winter sun.

We couldn't help but think, *What a beautiful place to die!* I remember one of the other parents remarking later that the young people were so very close to heaven when they died. Here Philip faced death—and yet the scene still gave a sense of great peace.

I think that in those times when we look

death straight in its ugly face, God provides for us a place to hide from our terror and pain, a place of stillness and tranquillity. And in that quiet hiding place, we at last understand something: Death cannot conquer love. Surrounded by darkness and sorrow, God's song still sings in our hearts.

> *For love cannot be buried,*
> *Nor crushed beneath death's pain;*
> *That's why my heart keeps singing*
> *Like robins in the rain.*
> —RUTH ALLA WAGER

We thank You, Lord, for surrounding us with the song of Your deliverance.

15

A Common Language

Blessed be the God. . .
who comforts us in all our tribulation,
that we may be able to comfort those
who are in any trouble,
with the comfort with which we ourselves
are comforted by God.
For as the sufferings of Christ abound in us,
so our consolation also abounds through Christ.
2 Corinthians 1:3–5

By 12:30 on the mountainside, a large crowd had gathered at the foot of the memorial cross, now decorated with flowers, ribbons, and the flags of the countries of the dead: Peruvian, America's Stars and Stripes, and the Spanish flag. Quietly, we waited for the priest to come, and finally, we saw the black-robed man laboring up the mountain.

I spoke the first words in Spanish: "We who are gathered here on this mountainside are one in our loss and grief, *Peruanos y Norte Americanos.*" I went on to speak from my heart of our joint loss and sorrow. I spoke of the common language of grief. I reminded them again of our oneness and that we are enabled by the love of our God to know His peace and His victory in spite of all.

When the service was over, I found that Peruvians are very emotional people. Men and women threw themselves upon us and wept. We wept with them. We cried with one mother who told us of her daughter's wedding the morning of the crash. She spoke of the bride and groom's happiness as they boarded the plane for their honeymoon in Lima. And here those newlyweds had died in the flames.

What a sad, traumatic time it was, a time I cannot even begin to describe. We shared our sorrow—not always with words but with the universal language of grief. Those simple mountain folks, descendants of the proud Incas, were one with us as together we furthered our acquaintance with grief.

Sometimes we're all too apt to look at the differences that separate us from each other. We don't dress the same or speak the same; our skins are different colors and we worship God in different ways. But around the world, human beings all cry in the very same way. We are one in our sorrow. And out of this oneness God can bring us strength for our days.

> *"How blessed the dead who die in the Lord*
> *For their works do follow them,"*
> > *thus saith His word.*
> *Though we cry out in anguish and dark is*
> > *the way,*
> *We know that He giveth us strength for*
> > *the day.*
> *This comforts the heart, though tears dim*
> > *the eyes*
> *Of him who on God's precious promise relies.*
> *So may we look upward, our hope fixed*
> > *on God,*
> *And follow the pathway our loved one*
> > *has trod.*
> > > —HILDEGARDE VAN WAVEREN

Help us, Lord, to reach out to all who are mourning. Hand in hand, help us to go forward, our hope fixed on You.

16

THE RAINBOW OF HOPE

Blessed be the God and Father
of our Lord Jesus Christ,
who according to His abundant mercy
has begotten us again to a living hope
through the resurrection of
Jesus Christ from the dead.
1 PETER 1:3

Someday I would like to go to Cuzco again. I know my sadness will be renewed, but I also know I will feel joy, for it was here in the presence and reality of death, in the quietness of Cuzco's great valley and the mountainside, that God worked a great miracle of healing in our hearts. We came boldly to this place to face the challenge between death and life. Life won!

Grief had thrown its clouds over us for two long years, but now the clouds parted. For the first time in many months, we saw beyond ourselves with clear eyes. We heard the words of Christ in John 4: "Behold, I say to you, lift up your eyes and look at the fields, for they are already white for harvest!" (verse 35). Peru, we realized, was not just the place where our son died; it was also a mission field hungry for the gospel.

In spite of everything, that summer was a wonderful time for each of us. Much healing came in Peru, and our hearts bonded with the Peruvian people. We met Tom and Carolyn Pace, a young missionary couple who will ever be dear to our hearts. In Chosica, Philip had attended their mission, and now they invited us to their new work in Juaja, in the Mantaro river valley, a valley rich in agriculture and in history. As a result of our acquaintance with the Paces, we have returned as summer missionaries to help them, both in 1976 and in 1997.

Still, we have found grief to be an acquaintance that lingers, waiting to pounce at unexpected times and places. Sometimes something so little will bring on a paroxysm of choking pain: a pair of shoes, a letter, a photograph.

I've often wondered why such simple things

can be so devastating. I remember especially one holiday season two years after Philip's death; during the Christmas assembly at the school where I taught, the band played "Little Drummer Boy." Suddenly, I saw my son as a sixth-grader playing the drums for that same song. I was completely broken as I blindly made my way from the auditorium. Another teacher, seeing me leave and recognizing the problem, came to be with me.

And yet, despite these moments of anguish, God's light has never failed us. In the darkness of grief in 1970, we could not foresee a dawn in our future. But in so many ways, God brought the comfort and glory of His new day, bringing us out of the darkness. Slowly and sometimes imperceptibly, the awful hopelessness gave place to acceptance and the assurance that our Heavenly Father actually was still in control. Clouds occasionally still darken our days, but we have come to know and to rejoice that there in the clouds God reaches out in love. Between the blackest, most towering thunderheads, we see the rainbow of eternal hope.

My prayer is that each of you will see that same rainbow.

THE DAWN OF HOPE

Claim the promise of the rainbow,
  Claim Him who sits upon the throne,
Claim His grace and peace and pardon,
  He your every need has known.
Claim the rainbow and the Master,
  Then claim His life for you beside.
Claim the fulness of the Saviour,
  And in Christ be satisfied.
                    —ORD L. MORROW

Lord, help us to claim the rainbow's promise. Show us the hope of Your Dawn.

PART II

GOOD-BYES

Death is not the only loss we face in our world. Life asks us to say all sorts of good-byes, for nothing in this world is permanent. Just as all too often we must say good-bye to those we love, so we also must say good-bye to our hopes and dreams.

But no matter how much practice we have at saying them, good-byes are never easy. After all, good-byes and loneliness go hand in hand. And loneliness is an aching void.

But Jesus will come to us when we feel so all alone. In His presence, we can find comfort for the empty days that follow our good-byes. And He will never leave us. . . .

1

SAYING GOOD-BYE TO A SPOUSE

You shall no longer be termed Forsaken,
Nor shall your land any more by termed Desolate;
But you shall be called Hephzibah,
and your land Beulah;
For the LORD delights in you,
And your land shall be married.
ISAIAH 62:4

How many times I have heard a widow complain: "The house is so very empty now. At night I reach out my arms, but he is not there to hold and comfort me. During the day I listen for his footsteps, but he does not come. I see a beautiful sunset, and I must have him share it with me. I call, but he does not hear. There are so many things I must share with him; I need to just talk with him. I desperately need his advice, but I face the future alone. I'm so very lonely!"

Widowers tell me much the same thing. He was dependent on his wife for so much. She was always there when he had a need, anticipating ways to help. Now he grows thin. He cannot cook as she did. His clothes need cleaning and mending. The house is so hard to keep clean. Without her it is no longer a home, and his arms are empty. He misses that comforting presence that he too often took for granted. He wishes he had expressed his love more often. Without a wife, he is so very incomplete and lonely.

I can well imagine that losing a spouse is one of the hardest good-byes to say. This person was a partner, the one with whom we shared life most intimately. Without this person nothing will ever be quite the same.

But Jesus can comfort even this desperate loneliness. If you are experiencing this sorrow, allow Him to fill the empty, aching hole in your heart. Remember, in His Word, our Lord promised to love us the way a spouse loves. He is our most intimate Partner, the One who will never leave us alone. Even in our loneliest, emptiest nights, He is there with us, holding us close with His arms of love.

Comfort for Those Who Grieve

Speak to my soul, dear Jesus,
Speak now in tenderest tone;
Whisper in loving kindness;
"Thou art not left alone."
Open my heart to hear Thee,
Quickly to hear Thy voice,
Fill my soul with Your presence,
And make my heart rejoice.

—Anonymous

When we long for that one person's loving presence,
come to us, Lord. Fill our hearts with Your love.

2

LOSING THE OLDER GENERATION

"For I have known him,
in order that he may command his children
and his household after him,
that they keep the way of the LORD,
to do righteousness and justice,
that the LORD may bring to Abraham
what He has spoken to him."
GENESIS 18:19

When my last uncle died, I was faced by the shocking reality that there were no more generations ahead of me. My generation is at the top of the list. And it is constantly fading away. I'm not just getting older; I'm getting old! Eternity lies ahead.

No matter how old we are, losing our parents is a special type of grief and loss. For one thing, parents have always been a vital fixture in our lives. They have always been there. They have nurtured us, supported us, disciplined us in the way we should go. Their arms comforted us. They stayed beside us in our sicknesses and problems. They shared the wonder of the world around us. They rejoiced in our successes and grieved with our defeats.

Often we have broken the umbilical cord of our childhood with a hurtful wrench. My mother called it "climbing fool's mountain." Whatever it is called, I know that after Christ came into my life, I knew no peace until I went to my father, asking for his forgiveness for the pain I had caused him. He gave me the assurance of his forgiveness.

I now know I was extremely blessed to have Daddy and Mum for my parents. Daddy died at sixty-six from cancer. Mum was a widow for thirty-five years until she, too, died at age ninety-four. I miss them, but the memories they left me are very rich.

Daddy was a stalwart man, honest and dependable. He was five-foot-five in height and weighed in at 115 pounds, but he could do the work of two husky men. Mum was known for her love for everyone; they called her Grammy in the family, in the church, and in the community. She, too, knew what it was to work hard without complaint, even though one of her legs was four inches shorter than the other. Strangely, her death was a time of inspiration, love, and joy, as the family gathered in her hospital room to sing and pray together. I pray that I may die with such victory.

Not only was I blessed by the parents God gave me, but He caused me to marry into a family where I was loved as one of their very own. I mourned when they left us: Dad at ninety-two and Mother at ninety-six. They touched my life with their love in so many ways. Their devotion to one another and to their Lord shaped my wife into the wonderful mother of our children. Her parents' love continues to flow into the lives of so many who have come after.

Even when the older generation leaves us behind, we can still feel their influence in our lives. We can take comfort in the heritage of love they have left us, a heritage we can pass on to our children and grandchildren.

Comfort for Those Who Grieve

So long Thy power has blest me,
*   sure it still will lead me on;*
Over moor and fen, over crag and torrent,
*   till the night is gone,*
And with the morn those angelic faces smile,
*   Which I have loved long since,*
*   and lost awhile.*
                              —John Newman

Thank You for our parents, Lord. Help us to pass their love on to those around us now.

3

EMPTY HEARTS
AND EMPTY ARMS

For as the sufferings of Christ abound in us,
so our consolation also abounds through Christ.
2 CORINTHIANS 1:5

They were a young couple. They had little of this world's goods, but they had each other and their little daughter. That little girl was greatly loved—yet after four years she was still like a baby. She didn't grow. She was blind. She could not talk.

They came to our church quite often. There they laid her beside them in the pew. Her thin arms waved feebly. She seemed to enjoy the music and the singing. All of our hearts went out to that couple and the child who could not live.

Cancer was destroying her eyes. Her days

were numbered, yet the parents' love never faltered. She was still their little girl whom they loved.

When she died, many said what a blessing it was that she was gone, for now the burden that crushed that family was lifted. But their grief was deep. Their loss was real. No matter the sacrifice, their lives had centered on that little one. Now the center was gone. Their lives and their arms were very empty.

I had that little girl's funeral. Looking back, I wish I had had more experience in bringing comfort. But in those days at the beginning of my ministry, I had suffered no great sorrows. I had had no need of comfort, and so I know that even though I did my best, I didn't truly understand the depth of their sorrow nor how to bring them the comfort for which they cried. Few of the skills and requisites of the ministry are learned in the classroom. They can only be learned by experience as we rub shoulders with the awesome and often sorrowful realities of life.

Those parents wanted to have that funeral be a very special time of remembrance of their child and their love of her. They especially wanted singing. The one I asked to sing was no stranger to grief; Reverend Enty had just recently lost one of his little twins. Though I lacked the discernment to see the depths of broken hearts, he brought the comfort so desperately needed as he sang out of his own grief:

When He cometh, when He cometh
To make up His jewels,
All His jewels, precious jewels,
His loved and His own.

As he sang, love poured out and encompassed those grieving parents. God gave great comfort. Tears flowed. From the depths of Reverend Enty's broken heart came the assurance that God cared. He was there! The God of all comfort brought the beginning of peace and purpose and healing down in the very depths of the darkness of despair. That little life had not been lived in vain. In her death we found the reality of a loving Heavenly Father. I, too, learned a lesson in compassion and understanding.

Losing a small child is one of the most bitter good-byes of all. It just doesn't seem right that this little one should have to experience death. How good, though, to know that children do not simply drop into death's fearsome darkness, to be lost and forgotten. No, they are as precious to God in death as in life. They are His jewels, and His tender love will keep them bright even in the dark night of death. And when the Dawn comes, we, too, will once again see them shine.

> *Little children, little children,*
> *Who love their Redeemer,*
> *Are the jewels, precious jewels,*
> *His loved and His own.*
>
> —GOSPEL CHORUS

Thank You, Lord, that our children, our greatest treasures, belong to You. Keep them bright through all eternity.

4

SAFE IN JESUS' ARMS

*I know whom I have believed
and am persuaded that He is able to keep
what I have committed to
Him until that Day.*
2 TIMOTHY 1:12

There are no easy answers when a child dies. Having lost my own son, I know now that pat answers bring no comfort. Losing someone from the younger generation goes against life's natural order. It is the one good-bye we never expected to say. What's more, it was our job as parents to keep this young life safe. We feel a sense of desperate failure mixed in with our good-bye.

But this I do know: Every child conceived is a part of God's plan and love. When those children are taken from us, we question His wisdom and His love. And sometimes we are even angry at Him for our loss. Always with us is the age-old question: Why?

I, too, have asked that question. I only know that God has proved His ability and desire to bring to pass what He has promised. He will bring comfort. He will be with us as we walk in the valley of the shadow of death. The Dawn will come when we not only shall see His purposes, but we shall see Him face-to-face! And then we shall once more greet and hold the little ones lost to us in the darkness of our night.

Our children's deaths do not make us failures as parents. We are not superheroes, capable of protecting our children from all life's dangers. From the moment they are born, they face a world of uncertainty and risk. The only rational option is to put them in God's hands—both in life and in death.

Your little ones are in good hands. God is keeping them safe until the Dawn. . .waiting for you to hold them once again in your arms. He can heal even this overwhelming grief, if you put your trust in Him.

THE DAWN OF HOPE

I heard the voice of Jesus say,
"Behold I freely give
The living water; thirsty one,
Stoop down, and drink, and live."

I came to Jesus, and I drank
Of that life-giving stream;
My thirst was quenched, my soul revived,
And now I live in Him.
—HORATIUS BONAR

We put our children in Your arms, Lord. Hold them close.

5

SAYING GOOD-BYE
TO OUR HOPES

As one whom his mother comforts,
So I will comfort you;
And you shall be comforted. . . .
ISAIAH 66:13

I knew of one who was forced to say good-bye to her greatest hope. We'll call her Kathy. After seven years of marriage Kathy's arms were still empty. Childless years stretched ahead of her and her husband. They continued to beseech God for a child.

Then a miracle. In the midst of their anxious yearning, there came hope that God was answering their prayers. Her joy grew as her body began to change with the demands of pregnancy. She and her pastor husband awaited the fulfillment of their prayers with almost delirious joy. A sense of wonder and thanksgiving gave a glow to their faces. They were filled with praise for the miracle in progress.

The months passed. Well-wishers offered congratulations and showers of gifts. Kathy and Norm were happy, but their doctor was mystified. There was something very wrong. Finally he was sure and he told those longing parents: Kathy was not pregnant! There was no baby, nor had there ever been! So strong was her desire for motherhood that she was having a false pregnancy.

We were close to them during that time, but I cannot begin to imagine the total devastation of that couple. In looking back, I'm sure our comprehension of their loss was very limited, although we grieved with them. The years of their waiting had been empty, but at least they still had hope. Now those hopes were torn from them, and their arms were so very empty. Darkness engulfed them as they said good-bye to their hopes and dreams.

During this period of darkness, God brought to them the opportunity of adoption. In their turn, two little ones became the babies Kathy was unable to conceive. In them she found the answer to her desire for motherhood. Neither those lost months filled with the couple's expectant joy nor the death of their hopes were forgotten. Now, though, they shared real joy that came in these children, conceived in the womb of another but theirs by the adoption of love.

The children are grown now. Kathy and Norm are proud grandparents. They have found the reality that "with God all things are possible." Adoption has given them a family, and they are fulfilled.

Kathy and Norm's story always reminds me that by adoption we, too, are accepted into the family of God. We are His children. His love has made this possible and we are accepted in the Beloved, one family for eternity.

And yet sometimes God asks us to let our dreams die. He asks us to say good-bye to all our plans and hopes for the future. But out of the dark night of disappointment and disillusionment, He will bring new life. Sometimes it is hard to wait. But until the Dawn. . .

THE DAWN OF HOPE

I heard the voice of Jesus say,
"Come unto Me and rest;
Lay down, thou weary one, lay down
Thy head upon My breast."

I came to Jesus as I was,
Weary and worn and sad;
I found in Him a resting place,
And He has made me glad.
—HORATIUS BONAR

Comfort us, Lord, when our dreams die. Make us glad again in Your hope.

6

A GOD WHO UNDERSTANDS

For He has not despised nor
abhorred the affliction of the afflicted;
Nor has He hidden His face from Him;
But when He cried to Him, He heard.
PSALM 22:24

Sometimes we're asked to say good-bye before we've even had a chance to say hello. . . .

You mothers who have experienced a miscarriage have suffered a very real grief and loss. Naturally, I am outside the intimate acquaintance you have with the death of an unborn baby. I can only speak from my role as pastor, grandfather, and father. My daughter had four miscarriages, and each time it was a real baby she lost. Her grief was deep and lasting.

But there were few who could truly weep with her. In far too many cases, the grief of miscarriage is a lonely grief, unacknowledged by the world. I, who lost a son, can understand in part the grief of a mother for her child, even though she has never held that baby in her arms. But do I fully understand? I am sure that I do not. I, too, am an observer. As a man I cannot enter into the mystery of motherhood. Nor can a husband, no matter how hard he tries, actually feel his wife's great sense of loss and emptiness. He, too, has had a part in creation; the child who died through miscarriage was also his—and yet he hasn't had the experience his wife had of actually having that baby as a part of him.

This is a time when a husband must make certain he gives all his love and attention to his wife. This is a time when a wife needs to know she is supported and cherished. It is a time to be one, a time to share and to understand one another as never before. It is a time to weep together and to heal together. It is time to turn to God together in prayer. God is the One who will carry you through it all, whole and fitted for the challenges of the future.

Denying that a pain exists will do no good. All of us in Christ's body the Church must reach out to those whose hearts are aching from this nearly invisible loss. We must acknowledge the pain of miscarriage, for as hard as it is to say, the word needs to be said: Good-bye. We need to help each other find the strength to say it and let go; when an unborn child dies, we must help each other acknowledge our loss before we can accept God's comfort and healing. If we want the dawn to come, we must first look around and accept that it is night.

But if you are being asked to say this particular good-bye, God does have healing and comfort for you. He understands your loss, even if no one else does. You will never forget this child you lost—but God will make you whole once more. He is with you in your sorrow. He feels your pain. And He will give you the strength to say good-bye.

The way is dark and the road is long;
Help me, dear Lord, for I cannot see!
Give me a light to guide me on;
Teach me with patience to follow Thee.
— MARGARET HOLLAND

Thank You, Lord, that no matter how dark and long our road seems, You are with us.

7

POOLS OF BLESSING

Wait on the LORD; Be of good courage,
And He shall strengthen your heart;
Wait, I say, on the LORD!
PSALM 27:14

Not all good-byes are caused by death or loss. Sometimes we grieve when a loved one is stricken with illness. We bid farewell then forever to our sense of safety. Death may not strike; but we will never again feel quite as secure.

Saying this good-bye can be painful. But God can use this experience to help us grow, as He did in the life of my third daughter, Faith. I'll let her tell you in her own words. . . .

My story is about our son, Philip, named after

my brother. My Philip is a curly-haired blond young man, who is twenty-four now; he's well and healthy and whole and a joy to us. When I was pregnant with Philip, we referred to him as "Blessing," and he has indeed been a blessing in our lives (although at times that blessing has driven us slightly crazy).

Early one November morning when Philip was four, I awoke to hear a strange noise coming from his bedroom. I hurried down the hall to his room, where I found him having a grand mal seizure. He was lying on his Sesame Street sheets, wearing his red, fuzzy sleeper; I can still see him at that moment. We called our doctor, who told us if Philip had another seizure to bring him to the emergency room.

We tucked a sleepy, bewildered Philip into bed with us, but it wasn't long before he had another seizure. We threw on our clothes, called still-sleeping friends to stay with Miranda, Philip's little sister, and hurried to the hospital. I remember on the way Philip asked me what was happening; I tried to explain to him, and he said, "What's a feizure, Mama?"

That morning, that day, was a nightmare. He was admitted to the hospital and continued to have seizures. I remember once when they sent out one of those code things over the hospital

PA system and all these people came rushing to his room. We weren't allowed in, and it seemed like more and more people in white coats hurried in. Eventually, someone ushered my husband Lee and me to a nurses' room, where once in a while a nurse or an aid would bring us cups of coffee. I was terrified.

Time became a blur. They set up a bed for me in Philip's room, and I stayed there while Lee made arrangements for work and for our daughter; he also called family and friends, asking for prayers. Meanwhile, Philip had tests and more tests.

A couple days passed and I was exhausted. The doctor had told us that he had ordered a CAT scan for the next morning, since they'd ruled out several things and were now looking for a brain tumor. Philip was also scared. More than once he soberly told me that he thought he was going to die.

That's a tough thing for a parent to hear. I pretended to be calm while I was with Philip, laughing with him and playing Legos with him, but inside I was falling apart. I desperately needed something to give me strength.

Knowing I was at the end of myself, Lee sent me home for the afternoon. I showered and put on clean clothes, but I couldn't sleep. I tried to pray and I couldn't. I cried a lot, all by myself in an empty house.

The day before, my brother-in-law had shown me a verse, and I kept reading it and rereading it, wanting to believe it: "When they walk through the Valley of Weeping it will become a place of springs where pools of blessing and refreshment collect after rains!" (Psalm 84:6, TLB). I was certainly in the valley of weeping, but I couldn't see any pools of blessing.

Finally, I started flipping through my Bible, looking for some comfort. The passage I opened up to was Matthew 17, verses 14–17, where a man approached Jesus and knelt before Him. "Lord, have mercy on my son," he said, "for he is an epileptic and suffers severely." And then Jesus said to the man, "Bring him here to Me."

I don't think I read any further then, where it told about Jesus healing the boy. I just knew that I had to bring my boy to Jesus, so I did. I knew that I was giving Philip to God—and that included letting him die if that was what God wanted. I said good-bye forever to my own control over Philip's life. Immediately, I was filled with the knowledge that God loved Philip even more than I loved him—and I loved him, still love him, more than I can express. But God loves him better and more and deeper than I ever can.

I suddenly knew that if God loved him that much, then I could trust God to do for Philip what was right; all I had to do was give my boy to God. I pictured Jesus sitting on a rock and I came into the picture carrying Philip in my arms. In my imagination, Philip was wearing those hospital pajamas they have for little kids, yellow with little animals printed on them. I walked to Jesus and laid Philip in His arms. "Good-bye," I whispered.

What a relief! It was going to be all right. I didn't know what *all right* was going to mean, but I knew, positively, that God would be taking care of Philip, that I didn't need to carry the burden anymore. God, with all His love, had His arms wrapped tight around my little boy and would keep him safe. I was filled with joy and peace and a real sense of God's presence.

I never slept that afternoon, but I went back to the hospital refreshed. As I was on my way to Philip's room, I met a friend who was coming to see us. She asked me how he was doing and I told her all our fears and all the bad news—and yet, while I was telling her, I kept smiling. "Faith, you sound happy!" she said. I told her that I *was* happy, because God loved Philip even more than I.

Philip didn't have a brain tumor. He was

diagnosed as having a seizure disorder. But the months that followed were among the most trying of my life. Through March of that year, Philip had many stays in the children's hospital. Sometimes he would have fifteen to twenty grand mal seizures in one day. One time he was in intensive care with IVs in both arms. Lee and I slept in chairs and waiting rooms and in the forerunner of the Ronald McDonald house. I cried when I spent our daughter Miranda's second birthday separated from her. During these few months, Philip also had herpangina, fifths disease, throat infections, and chicken pox! While all this was going on, our daughter Miranda had chronic ear infections; we had her to the doctor's or the emergency room every other week. She had a horrible case of chicken pox and would only sleep while I was rocking her. She, also, had a brief hospital stay. And Lee and I both had jobs that we were trying to get to now and then. It was an awful winter.

I can't say I was joyous and happy all that time. Mostly I was exhausted. But all through it, I felt a strong sense of God's presence, of His love and His caring. I had let go of my own control over life—and in return, not only did I have a realization of the depths of God's love for Philip, but I also realized that He loved me that much, too. Through it all I felt upheld and at peace. God was with me and I knew it. I told Philip that Jesus was holding him in His arms.

An artist friend of mine painted a picture for me that still hangs in my dining room. It shows a four-year-old Philip sitting on Jesus' lap. Jesus' face is full of love and laughter as He holds Philip close. Whenever I need to be reminded of Christ's love for my child, I look at that painting.

The times I've felt closest to God have been those times when I was at the end of my own coping skills, when I reached down into myself and there was nothing left to carry me through, and so I turned to God. At those times, God's response to me has been wonderful and I have felt blessed. But nowhere does God say He will do that for me only when I have reached the end of myself. All that love and support from God are always available to me, during desperate times and during good times and during everyday times. Those pools of blessing and refreshment that I was promised in Psalm 84:6 were right there in the Valley of Weeping. I was blessed and refreshed then—and I still am whenever I remember the lesson I learned that day.

Philip never had another seizure after we left the children's hospital in March that winter. I'm sure the doctors would tell you they finally got the right combination of medications to control the seizures, and that he eventually grew out of them. I don't know. I don't know how God did it. But I do know I said good-bye to my son and gave him to God—and he was healed. Praise the Lord!

—FAITH STEWART

I'm beginning to realize that whatever God does is a miracle! I suppose to Him miracles are just the expression of His person and power, but from our viewpoint God's ways are beyond our comprehension.

Is God asking you to say good-bye to something in your life today? It might be health or independence, a job or a home, a relationship or your sense of who you are. Whatever it is, good-byes are never easy. But when we finally let go, when we place whatever the thing is in God's hand, then we'll be amazed by the miracles God will do. We, too, will find those pools of blessing and refreshment.

I know not what the future holds,
What lies along my trail;
I only know that God is real,
His power can never fail.

THE DAWN OF HOPE

I know not what the hours may bring,
*   What pain, what grief, what task;*
I only know God's help is mine,
*   If I but stop and ask.*

I only know that God is Good,
*   Forever and for aye;*
I know but this—and it's enough:
*   I'll walk with Him today.*
                    —RUTH ALLA WAGER

Lord, when we find ourselves in the Valley of Weeping, remind us to look for Your pools of blessing.

8

A SIMPLE PRAYER

But as many as received Him,
to them He gave the right to
become children of God,
to those who believe in His name.
JOHN 1:12

We got the news on our way home from our vacation: Dorothy was dead. For nearly forty years she had been a very special person in our lives. Now she was with the Lord and her family wanted me to have the funeral service. I felt both honored and humbled, for she was one of God's great ones.

We had met Dorothy the first Sunday we became pastors of the Wesleyan Methodist Mission in Oakland, New York. She was an extremely shy person, and she said hardly a word as we greeted her after the church services. But each Sunday she was there. I sensed she had something to ask me, and finally she got up her nerve to ask if she could come to the parsonage to talk with us. We agreed to meet the following Tuesday evening.

Tuesday evening she arrived, but she seemed unable to begin the conversation. Once she got started, however, it poured out of her: When she was ten years of age, a schoolteacher had asked her if she believed in Jesus. She did and she assured the teacher of that fact. "Then," the teacher said, "you are born again. You are a Christian." Dorothy wanted to believe that, but she felt no change.

Several years passed. She was in her teens when revival meetings were held in her church. Again, she sought the assurance of her salvation. As she knelt at the altar, she was asked, "Do you believe Christ died for your sins?" She did and again she was assured that she was indeed a Christian. But still she could not believe the truth. She gave up going to church. She married and had several children. The hunger to know Christ's peace did not leave her, however.

Now, as I talked with her about God's plan of salvation, I asked her if she would like to pray once more for her salvation. I prayed first. Then she prayed, "Dear Lord, I know You can save me." It was a good start, but she wasn't quite on solid ground yet and nothing changed. I urged her to take the leap of faith and to pray, "Lord, I know You *have* saved me!"

Once that prayer of faith was uttered, Dorothy was changed for the rest of her life. She never wavered. After we left the area, we received ten- to twelve-page letters bursting with praise for the way God was working in her heart and life. A fearful woman, she had feared the dark before she knew her Lord; now all fear was gone. She was set free. She remained a shy, reserved woman, but her pen sang in letters and poetry. She was one of God's great people whom you had to know to truly appreciate. God has always used the weak things of this earth to proclaim His power and glory, and Dorothy was no exception.

Now Dorothy is dead, but like Enoch of old she still speaks. That funeral was a glory time as I thanked God for Dorothy. What a great witness she was to her family. Knowing people like this makes it easy to tell people of the coming Dawn when all tears are washed away and all things are made new. Dorothy is waiting up there with her Lord and Savior. He was, after all, just a simple prayer away.

Some good-byes are easier to say than others. It's that simple prayer that makes all the difference. When Christ's Dawn comes, we will no longer say good-bye. Instead, that wonderful morning will echo with joyous greetings. I don't know about you, but I can hardly wait.

There is a gentle voice that's calling,
Softly calling from above;
There is a gentle Friend who's waiting
Just to give His wondrous love.
When the days are dark and dreary,
When the clouds obscure the blue;
You may know that He is waiting,
That His love is calling you.

He is calling, He is calling,
If you listen you will hear;
If you heed Him, if you need Him,
You will find Him always near.
—LOUISE E. STAIRS

Thank You, Lord, that in You our good-byes are not forever.

9
WHY?

For since by man came death,
by Man also came the
resurrection of the dead.
For as in Adam all die,
even so in Christ all shall be made alive.
1 CORINTHIANS 15:21–22

I enjoyed the years I spent pastoring, not only because of the challenge of the gospel, but also because of the many wonderful people in the churches I served. Nelson and Arlah were two of those special ones. They were the first couple I united in marriage after my wife and I were married. During those five years of our first full-time pastorate in Black Creek, New York, we came to appreciate them. They were people easy to love, and even after we left that church our friendship continued.

We had much in common. They were near our ages. We had five children, and they had five about the ages of ours. They were a family loved by many, at church and at work. They had the ability to make others feel loved and worthy; their Christian life was real and consistent. We enjoyed their fellowship.

Near the time of their fifteenth wedding anniversary, tragedy came to Nelson and Arlah and their family. On vacation with their family in the Adirondacks, their car was involved in an accident when an approaching driver apparently had a heart attack. Nelson swerved off the road, but their car was still hit head-on. He and Arlah and their second child were killed. The others, including the baby, were hospitalized but recovered. Their grandmother was given the responsibility to care for them and raise them. Although she was crippled by arthritis, the Lord was her strength and guide, and she did a remarkable job raising those children.

But we are still left with the question, "Why?" Why do we have to say good-bye to wonderful people like Nelson and Arlah? Why does God allow these tragic things to happen? And why do they happen to God's people? What was gained for the kingdom by taking that father and mother and sister away from their family?

I don't know and I cannot even guess why. But I find comfort in the fact that my God makes no mistakes, and His hands are upon our lives. We are certain that in spite of everything, even when the word "good-bye" makes our hearts break, in God's time, He will demonstrate His love and His purpose. Romans 8:28 has been proven true over and over in my life: "All things work together for good to those who love God, to those who are the called according to His purpose."

We don't understand why bad things happen, Lord. But we trust You to keep us eternally safe.

10
No Shortcuts

*There is a way that
seems right to a man,
But its end is the way of death.*
PROVERBS 14:12

We sing, "There's a great Day coming." And we want to be part of that Day, the Day when we will never have to say good-bye again—but what can we do in the meantime? In spite of our every effort, sorrow continues to encompass us. Grief seems to be our lot. There must be a way out of our troubles, but we fail to find the Way.

My children still laugh about the time I thought I had found a shortcut on our way home. I don't know what went wrong with my plan, but we ended up at the end of a very rough dirt road in someone's onion patch. We lost miles and over an hour getting home that night. "There is a way which seems right to a man. . . ."

When sorrows come, often our most important activity seems to be the continual asking, "Why? Why this? Why now? Why me?" I'm sure we'd do well to ask another "why?" Why did the wonder of God's creation turn into the darkness of sin and death? What happened to that time when love ruled all decisions, when good-byes were not forever? In that time, man and woman were certain of God's interest in them, and so they had no needs that were not satisfied by God's lavish provision.

John says in his first epistle, "God is love." He is not only love, but He is One whose love directs all of His actions. The creation of all things was an act of love. But when Adam and Eve sinned, they shattered the beautiful whole-ness God had given them. They left us with the broken pieces, the sorrows and frustration and hatred that still curse our world.

Like Adam and Eve, we, too, have sinned and fallen short of God's glory. And death forces us to say good-bye all too often. Death separates us from those we need and love, just as sin separates us from our God. But of this we are certain—our hope is in the death and resurrection of our Lord and Savior, Jesus Christ. Through Christ, God has an eternal plan for each one of our lives, a plan that continues unchanged no matter how many times we are forced to say good-bye.

But the only road back to loving fellowship with the Father and His creation leads through Calvary. There are no shortcuts.

> *Because of Calvary, today I have found joy,*
> *A joy that will not tarnish or grow*
> *dim;*
> *A joy that will not perish in the using,*
> *But constant, radiant, glows as some*
> *bright gem.*
>
> *Because of Calvary, oh, Lord, no longer I*
> *delay;*
> *Because of all Thy love has done for me,*
> *Today I yield my life, my love, my all,*
> *Thine evermore, because of Calvary!*
> —HARRIETTE S. PARKER

Thank You, Lord, that through Calvary You turned death into an open door that leads us to Your presence.

PART III

GOD OF ALL COMFORT

We cannot escape the good-byes that fill our lives. But let us now turn to the source of all comfort: God, our Heavenly Father.

The apostle Paul wrote, "Blessed be the God and Father of our Lord Jesus Christ, the Father of mercies and God of all comfort, who comforts us in all our tribulation" (2 Corinthians 1:3–4). There is no grief that we suffer that God cannot comfort. What is more, He will enable us to pass His comfort on to others who are hurting. . . .

1

THIRSTING FOR COMFORT

Jesus stood and cried out, saying,
"If anyone thirsts,
let him come to Me and drink.
He who believes in Me,
as the Scripture has said,
out of his heart will flow
rivers of living water."
JOHN 7:37–38

"Those who sow in tears shall reap in joy" are the words of our Lord in Psalm 126:5. But can there ever be true joy in the morning when a part of our very being is missing? Isn't that expecting too much? Yet God promises that all things are possible even when our arms and hearts are empty.

Sometimes Christians seem to feel that if

they're sad, that means they lack faith. They read the Bible, and they believe that the promises of joy and hope should totally erase all our sadness. I am acquainted with a family who feels that Christians should not weep over the loss of a loved one. At the death of their son, they displayed no outward signs of grief. When the father died, the service was a time for hilarious memories. They did not allow themselves a time of grieving.

The truth is, however, that sorrow is real; and the Bible acknowledges human anguish and suffering. Certainly we are not to grieve as those who have no hope—but is there anything wrong with expressing our sorrow when one we love is taken from us, never to be seen again in this world? Christ grieved for His cousin, John the Baptist. When His friend Lazarus died, He wept with Mary and Martha. As He looked over the city of Jerusalem, He wept for a people who had turned their backs on hope and were spiritually dead.

You can be certain that when Jesus sees your great loss and need, He cries for you. He cares. He expects us to grieve, for grieving is a part of God's process of healing and comfort.

Our vulnerability to sorrow is also one mark of our ability to be what God wants—a comforter of the comfortless. From our broken hearts come the seeds of our own compassion for others in their distress. Whenever my wife and I hear a report of another plane crash, we lift our hearts in prayer for those who mourn. This is the way that we who have lost so much become rich by God's grace. We have gained the riches of understanding that enable us to bring help to others in their darkness.

I, too, know the longing for comfort when all is dark and you thirst for something or someone to satisfy that void within your heart. And that painful knowledge is a gift that helps me comfort others. God not only answers my thirst for comfort; His comfort also flows through me to others. That is why we can have the courage to trust Him even when our hearts are empty and thirsting.

In pastures green? Not always; sometimes He
Who knoweth best, in kindness leadeth
me
In many ways where heavy shadows be.
Out of the sunshine warm and soft and
bright—
Out of the sunshine into the darkest night,
I oft would faint with sorrow and
affright,
Only for this—I know He holds my hand;

THE DAWN OF HOPE

So whether in the green or desert land
I trust although I may not understand.
           —REV. JOHN F. CHAPLAIN

Thank You, Lord, that You put rivers of living water
inside our hearts.

2

TRUST:

THE BEGINNING OF COMFORT

That we may be able to comfort those
who are in any trouble,
with the comfort with which we ourselves
are comforted by God.
2 CORINTHIANS 1:4

My granddaughter, three-year-old Micaela, ran to me and wrapped her arms about my legs in a fierce hug. Looking up into my face, she declared, "I love you, Grandpa, because you love me." She knows the way to this old man's heart. Isn't it wonderful to have such an open, childlike trust and confidence and love! I probably don't need to say that I love that little bright-eyed girl with all my heart.

We can come to God with the same trust and love: We love Him because He loves us. This is where our comfort begins—in the realization that God is love and He cares for us. The apostle John looked up into the Father's face with a child's confidence and declared, "We love Him because He first loved us" (1 John 4:19).

Trouble starts early in our lives, whether it be a stubbed toe or a disappointment. That's when most of us found we could go to those who loved us with our woes and hurts. We went with confidence that they would help and give a loving kiss "to make it all better."

As we grew into adolescence, we found life was far more complex, and our hearts broke over hidden "crushes." We were overcome with our feelings, and we felt no one really cared. With adulthood came other problems: Wrong choices bring guilt; broken promises wound the very depths of our beings; loneliness like a wall shuts out the light and the joy of living. Death is so final and grief so dark.

But it is in these situations we need to look up and declare, "Father, I love You. You love me. You care." We can be very sure that no matter how great or how deep the hurt or the aching void within us, God does care. He has comfort for us—and when our grief is over and the morning comes, we will find that we understand the suffering of others far better, and our hearts will reach out to comfort them.

That's the reward for receiving comfort: We pass on what we have received so that others are comforted, too. After all, that's what comfort is all about, whether from God or from others: knowing someone cares and understands and gives his or her support. We are loved even when we feel the most unlovable.

When Jesus knew the end was very near, He asked for the apostles' confidence and in return gave them comfort. "Let not your heart be troubled; you believe in God, believe also in Me" (John 14:1).

Trust. That's the beginning of comfort. The confidence in our heavenly Father's love, that same confidence we learned through our own troubles, is the comfort we have to share with others.

> *I asked for strength that I might achieve;*
> *He made me weak that I might obey.*
> *I asked for health that I might do greater*
>   *things;*
> *I was given grace that I might do better*
>   *things.*

The Dawn of Hope

I asked for riches that I might be happy;
I was given poverty that I might be wise.
I asked for power that I might have the
praise of men;
I was given weakness that I might feel the
need of God.
I asked for all things that I might enjoy
life;
I was given life that I might enjoy all
things.
I received nothing that I asked for, all that
I hoped for,
My prayer was answered.

—Anonymous

Help us to trust You, Lord, when hard times come.

3

GOD'S TOUCH

"Comfort, yes, comfort My people!"
says your God.
"Speak comfort to Jerusalem."
ISAIAH 40:1–2

In this Scripture, God is shouting through the prophet Isaiah His great desire to comfort His people. In the same way He longs to comfort and heal us.

The woman in Matthew 9 had witnessed the draining of her life from her for so many years. Doctors had drained her of her money as well, but they brought her no healing or comfort (see Mark 5:25–26). She was drained of hope also; she doubted she would ever live a life without suffering. Then Jesus came her way and she experienced hope again. And so she reached out her hand and touched His robe. "Jesus turned around, and when He saw her He said, 'Be of good cheer, daughter; your faith has made you well.' And the woman was made well from that hour" (Matthew 9:22). The circumstances in our lives are probably different—but many times we, too, have stood in need of the comfort-giving touch of our God.

In Christ, God won the victory for each of us. In Christ, the fear of death is removed. In Christ, our future is secure. In Christ, we see the end of our warfare against sin. In Christ, our iniquity is pardoned. In Christ, we can now come boldly to God's throne of grace and mercy. In Christ, we have the assurance of His presence in all our need, for He is the God of all comfort. God is definitely in control!

The dictionary defines comfort as relief from sorrow or distress. It is help and support, aid and consolation. To find comfort is to be cheered in the time of grief or trouble. Comfort brings solace and consolation.

God's comfort restores and heals the hurting soul. It lifts the crushed and broken spirit. It brings again a sense of worth and purpose when all seems empty and dark. Comfort is the touch of God when we thought we were alone in our night. It is the promise that the dawn is on its way.

If you are now walking in a place of grief or heartache, if you feel alone, separated from love and security, God has comfort for you. When the news comes that your sickness will not be healed, God gives strength for your days and light for your valley. When you face the termination of your job, when the good-byes you have to say are bitter and painful, God is there with you. All you have to do is reach out and touch Him.

I hear the Savior say,
"Thy strength indeed is small!
Child of weakness, watch and pray,
Find in Me thy all in all."
—ELVINA M. HALL

Show us how to touch You, Lord. Be our all in all.

4

HOPE IN THE DARKNESS

The LORD is good,
A stronghold in the day of trouble;
And He knows those who trust in Him.
NAHUM 1:7

Comfort was in God's hand when He touched a man named Park in the darkness of a West Virginia coal mine as the rocks collapsed about him.

Park came to Houghton College while I was a student there. (We considered him an older man. He was around thirty at the time!) He came to college to prepare for the work the Lord was calling him to. When Park was in his early teens, he had joined his father and brothers and went to work in the coal mine. His mother had hoped for better things for him, but he quit school and went down into the darkness of the pit. The years passed, and he lived in sin. Down through those years, his mother prayed for protection and salvation for her family—especially for her boy, Park.

Then came the day that he and another young man were sent to "rob pillars." The mine roof was supported by large sections of unmined coal, and from time to time, those pillars were mined for the coal in them. It was dangerous work, since no one knew for sure just how much coal could be safely removed. On that day, Park was shoveling coal into a car, when suddenly everything collapsed. The coal car was twisted into an unrecognizable heap of scrap metal. The floor heaved and the roof came down.

The other young man was crushed. Park still lived in a small space beside the coal car, but almost every bone in his body was broken. Still conscious, he knew he was about to die, and he wasn't ready. There in the darkness he cried out to God, promising Him that if he could escape he would do anything God asked him to do.

God heard his desperate cry; Park was finally rescued, though no one could understand how he had escaped death. Months of recovery lay ahead, however. One arm was gone, and he was covered with scars. But he was a changed man.

He remained true to his promise and began preparing for the work set before him.

I was privileged to have known Park. His life ministry was as chaplain in Leavenworth Prison. He had found comfort in the reality of God's presence when all was hopeless, and now he brought hope to many hopeless men. God had comforted Park in that dark coal mine. He brought Park hope that the dawn would come. And God stayed with Park down through the years.

When our lives collapse around us, God can bring us hope, just as He did for Park.

Abide with me! Fast falls the eventide.
The darkness deepens; Lord, with me
    abide!
When other helpers fail and comforts flee,
Help of the helpless, oh, abide with me.
        —HENRY F. LYTE

On our own, Lord, we are helpless. Give us hope, we pray.

5

A BULWARK OF LOVE

"The eternal God is your refuge,
And underneath are the everlasting arms."
DEUTERONOMY 33:27

In the winter of 1998, the ocean current El Niño was blamed for the relentless storms that one after another buffeted the California coast. Sea walls were swept away. Homes fell victim to the powerful waves. Life was often in jeopardy. It was a fearful time.

Although you may not live in California, I'm sure some of you know the same feeling of uncertainty. Every conceivable storm of trial and tribulation seems pitted against you. The winds of change threaten your stability. Raging waves of anger and recrimination have been released against you. Your strength and resistance are eroding away. The clouds and darkness of despair cover the sun of hope. The foundations of your very existence crumble beneath you.

When it seems you can take no more, the One who created all things is able to aid you in your hour of need. When the storm of our grief overwhelms us, we often fail to accept God's hiding places, for we cannot or do not think as clearly as we ought. But God is there. God is at work and God is faithful; He will provide a bulwark of love where we can take refuge and weather the storm.

Jesus calls to us in love, "Come to Me, all you who labor and are heavy laden, and I will give you rest" (Matthew 11:28).

> *But recently I felt too tired*
> *To climb upon His knee—*
> *And then I felt His tender arms*
> *Reach down and cradle me.*
> *At last my heart can understand*
> *The meaning and the truth*
> *Of words I've heard so often said*
> *From earliest days of youth.*
> *I know those Everlasting Arms*
> *Are underneath me here;*

With such great strength surrounding me
What can my spirit fear?
                    —RUTH ALLA WAGER

Be our bulwark against life's storms, dear Lord.
Cradle us in Your love.

6

OUR SECURITY BLANKET

"If you love Me, keep My commandments.
And I will pray the Father,
and He will give you another Helper,
that He may abide with you forever—
the Spirit of truth,
whom the world cannot receive,
because it neither sees Him nor knows Him;
but you know Him,
for He dwells with you and will be in you.
I will not leave you orphans;
I will come to you."
JOHN 14:15–18

I have heard many children cry, "I want my blankie," when they are tired and overwhelmed by life. A child has so much to fear: nighttime, dogs, monsters, bugs, strangers. Some of my grand-children have even feared innocent things like cats and butterflies, balloons and clowns. They needed a security blanket to get them through their days. . .and their nights.

We smile at their insistence—but just be-cause we are adults doesn't mean that from time to time we, too, don't need our "blankie." No mat-ter how much we may try to avoid the hard times, the realities of life must be faced. We are weak. We mourn. And when we mourn, we need comfort. We need strength to continue on.

As a kid, I could do all kinds of scary things if I had someone with me. Walking home in the dark was one of those frightening things that lost its terror when my brother walked with me. Now I lose my fear when I hear Jesus say, "Even though the way may seem so awfully dark and scary at first, you won't have to walk alone."

Jesus reminds us in the Beatitudes: "Blessed are those who mourn, for they shall be com-forted." And the night before His crucifixion He reminded His friends again that He wasn't going to leave them without a Comforter. The Greek word used here for Comforter is *Paraclete*—One who walks beside us, no matter how dark and scary our path.

Those were frightening days after Jesus died.

The disciples saw enemies all about them. Rumors were rife. Unanswered questions burned within them. But then came the dawn of the realization that their Lord was indeed risen from the dead. Their hope was renewed. But still they faced an uncertain future until He unfolded the plan He had for them. Those uneducated, common folk were the forerunners of those who would go into all the world and preach the gospel. They put into action all their Lord had begun!

When you face the enormity of days filled with grief, when the task is far greater than your strength, think of those disciples. Christ had been their constant Companion. They knew Him and His power, and they depended on Him. Now He was telling them to go and do His work. And then He left them.

But on the Day of Pentecost, the Holy Spirit descended upon them in power. The Spirit filled them. God was not only with them; God dwelt within them! In the Comforter's powerful presence, they went forth to conquer the world for God.

God did not leave them comfortless or without strength. Nor will He ignore your need.

Breathe on me, Breath of God,
Until I am wholly Thine,
Until this earthly part of me
Glows with Thy fire divine.
                    —EDWIN HATCH

Fill us with Your Spirit, Lord. Comfort us. Make us Yours. Use us for Your kingdom.

7

THE COMFORT OF MEMORY

The memory of the righteous is blessed.
PROVERBS 10:7

We are saved by God's unlimited grace. With this gift we make it through the trials and tribulations of this life. In His grace lies our hope.

God also has another gift that He has given humanity—the gift of memory. Memory causes us to face the sins and failures of life that we might be forgiven and be made new in Christ. And memory is one of our greatest means of healing and encouragement as we face a life without our loved one.

When Philip was killed, an acquaintance expressed her thought that it must be far worse to lose a child at sixteen than when a child is three, as was her little girl when she died. Yet as we talked, I realized her memories of that little one were vivid. Memory made her alive even after many years. I assured her that I believed that there is no good time to lose a child—but she could thank God for the memory that kept that little girl alive.

Memory, like any gift given in love, is "a sweet-smelling aroma, an acceptable sacrifice, well pleasing to God" (Philippians 4:18). Memory heals and encourages us to face the future. Memory does not ignore the fact that our loved one is dead, but it does give us a continuing hold on that beloved life.

The vacuum left by the departure of our loved one is somewhat filled by remembering. Those memories can and should be the greatest tribute and memorial we can pay our loved one. Properly used, memory can lift us above the finality of death. Memory reveals the dawn of God's light in the darkest of nights.

At a recent funeral, six sons and their families gathered to say good-bye to their mother and grandmother. She became a reality as we shared memories. One son told of her lifelong vanity concerning high-heel shoes; she refused to wear anything else. When her son found her dead at her desk, she was still wearing her red high heels!

Another son reminded us of her love of music and singing. He then proceeded to lead the mourners in hymn after hymn that he and his brothers had learned at her knee as she sang to them.

The tiny details that make our loved one real, the ordinary days together, the extraordinary moments of love and joy, the memories of all these give us comfort when death comes between us. I know that the memories of our son's accomplishments, his development, and maturity continue to sustain us. And even more, the memories of Philip's everyday part in our family keep him alive as a real person. He loved to tease his mother and sisters—but how they loved him. He was a boy with an unswerving loyalty to his family, his friends, and his God.

Our memories of Philip are without price, for we loved that boy so much. We were just beginning to get acquainted with the young man he was becoming when he died. As I grow older, I'm excited about seeing him again—alive!

To you I would say, treasure your memories. As a memorial of what was, they can't be beat. And as a light in the darkness, they will lead you toward the Dawn.

And I know, though the silence hurts me
　　sore
And still to my longing his voice is
　　　dumb,
He has only "beaten me home" once more;
He has "gone ahead to open the door,"
　　And he's waiting there for me to come.
　　　　　　　—ANONYMOUS

Thank You, Lord, for the gift of memory. Keep our loved ones alive in our hearts until we see them again —in heaven!

8

COMFORT FOR EVERY GRIEF

When the poor and needy seek water,
and there is none,
and their tongue faileth for thirst,
I the LORD will hear them,
I the God of Israel
will not forsake them.
ISAIAH 41:17 KJV

When I was studying art, we were instructed to use one twelve-inch by eighteen-inch piece of light cardboard and construct a container for a raw egg so that it could be dropped from a height of thirty feet without being broken. It was a rather exciting time when we were ready to test our "masterpieces." Newspapers were spread and we went up to the third-floor landing of a stairwell. As the stairway wound upward, a space about twenty-four inches wide was open to the floor below. Down that space we dropped our eggs. The newspapers were very, very necessary. It took a lot of planning, but I'm happy to say my hard work paid off: I successfully created a bulwark for that fragile egg.

When we consider how God erects bulwarks of protection for us in our time of testing, we are amazed how well He planned and prepared them all. You might say that every comfort is a "custom job," customized to our special need. God is not too great to know us and our hurts.

Grief has many faces. Some of us mourn the children and other loved ones we have lost. Meanwhile, others grieve for the love they never even had a chance to experience or for the dream that died before they saw it come to fruition. But many are the faces of comfort God has, one for each and every face of sorrow.

We are a part of that equation of comfort. Whatever pain we have experienced, no matter how small or seemingly insignificant, if we give it to God, He can use it to help another who is in the same situation. We are each an essential link in a long chain of comfort, and our feeblest effort is important. A thoughtful word, a loving act of kindness, a touch, a hug are so simple yet so very effective. When we show we care, we show others that God cares, too. When we are with others in their sorrow, we demonstrate God's presence.

> *We reach our hand to Him, and find*
> *A blessed answer to our fear;*
> *His hand holds ours; we hear His voice,*
> *"Fear not, for I am here."*
> —DINNIE McDOLE HAYES

Thank You, Lord, that Your comfort is strong enough to protect our hearts from every grief. Help us to pass Your comfort on to others.

9

A LOVING PRESENCE

*My God shall supply all
your need according to
his riches in glory by Christ Jesus.*
PHILIPPIANS 4:19

As outsiders to a deep loss, a part of our problem is that we don't know what to say or do. I have always felt so uncertain and ineffectual in times like these.

What do I say?

What not to say?

Will I cause greater hurt?

How can I help and comfort?

Despite our inadequacy and insufficiency, God's Word assures us: "And God is able to make all grace abound toward you, that you, always having all sufficiency in all things, may have an abundance for every good work" (2 Corinthians 9:8; see also 3:5).

My supply comes not from myself; instead I am invited to draw on the bank account of Christ Himself! The resources of heaven are mine—not for my selfish glory, but to do the work and will of the Father.

My mind may be poverty-stricken, lacking wisdom; I may not know how to help—but my God has an abundant supply of comfort for the problem right now. This is not a supply just for preachers either. It is available for all of God's people who in obedience seek to serve those who need help and understanding. In receiving comfort, we are enriched to give comfort.

When you are unsure, love and be loving! You can't go too far wrong. God will always bring comfort from a loving presence.

When our daughter Ellyn lost her babies, I grieved for the grandchildren I never had the privilege to hold, but my greatest grief was for my child and her loss and grief. I didn't know what to say or do to comfort her. But I hope she felt our love and was comforted by our understanding. We prayed, and we let Ellyn and Paul know we prayed.

Sometimes all we can do is pray for each

other. But our prayer taps heaven's power. God will send His Comforter to help those whose hearts are broken.

The Comforter has come,
   the Comforter has come!
Holy Ghost from heaven—
   the Father's promise given;

O spread the tidings 'round wherever man
   is found—
The Comforter has come!

—ANONYMOUS

Thank You, Lord, for Your Comforter. Thank You that He supplies all our needs.

10

COMFORT SHARED

"Give, and it will be given to you:
good measure, pressed down, shaken together,
and running over will be put into your bosom.
For with the same measure that you use,
it will be measured back to you."
LUKE 6:38

Roy is a businessman who loves the Lord and shows it by loving others. He loves to visit anyone who is hurting and lonely, and he especially appreciates his ministry with the old folks in nursing homes.

Recently he went to the local nursing home at their dinnertime. The residents sat at their tables, isolated and desolate, staring at their plates. Roy walked among them, touching them on their hands or shoulders while saying kind words of encouragement and love. When he left a few minutes later, the atmosphere was transformed. Residents smiled and spoke to each other. Someone had shown them that he cared.

Why are we reticent to love those who so desperately need to know that "God is our refuge and strength, a very present help in trouble" (Psalm 46:1)? We excuse ourselves by saying we feel shy or awkward or embarrassed. But how little it takes on our part to offer love to someone who is alone and hurting.

A little girl named Janet had died. She was greatly missed by her friend next door. That friend asked her mother if she could go outside. When she came back into the house some time later, her mother asked where she had been so long. Her daughter answered, "I've been over to Janet's house."

"But why would you go there?" her mother wondered.

"I went to make Janet's mama feel better."

"But how could you comfort her?"

"I just climbed up in her lap and she hugged me tight. Then we cried together."

This is a story of a very wise little girl. She identified with another's sorrow, and she demonstrated her compassion. So many hurting people are waiting for the simple sense that someone understands and cares.

When you give yourself for others, use a large measure if you really want to get a great blessing from that service. "As you sow so shall you reap," is a God-given truth. The growth is in the seed, but the planting is done by a human hand that reaches out to sow. Because God loves you, He will comfort you, and you will comfort others. We cannot outgive God.

If I can stop one heart from breaking,
I shall not live in vain;
If I can ease one life the aching,
Or cool one pain,
Or help one fainting robin
Unto his nest again,
I shall not live in vain.

—EMILY DICKINSON

Help us to share Your comfort, Lord. We don't want to live in vain.

11

Conduits for God's Peace

Then He arose and rebuked the wind,
and said to the sea, "Peace be still!"
And the wind ceased
and there was a great calm.
Mark 4:39

A small boy was awakened by the flash and crash of a summer thunderstorm, and he cried out in fear. His father picked him up and comforted him, reminding him not to be afraid, for Jesus loved him and He was there.

"But," sobbed the little boy, "right now I need someone with skin on."

Isn't this what James is talking about when

he says, "If a brother or sister is naked and destitute of daily food, and one of you says to them, 'Depart in peace, be warmed and filled,' but you do not give them the things which are needed for the body, what does it profit?" (James 2:15–16). Yes, what good does it profit, when our hearts are not in our comforting? What good is it to be a Christian and not be one who reaches out with our faith and deeds to others? God needs us to "put skin on" His love.

In 2 Corinthians 1:3–7, Paul lays the foundation of God's purposes for comfort:

> *Blessed be the God and Father of our Lord Jesus Christ, the Father of mercies and God of all comfort, who comforts us in all our tribulation, that we may be able to comfort those who are in any trouble, with the comfort with which we ourselves are comforted by God. For as the sufferings of Christ abound in us, so our consolation also abounds through Christ. Now if we are afflicted, it is for your consolation and salvation, which is effective for enduring the same sufferings which we also suffer. Or if we are comforted, it is for your consolation and salvation. And our hope for you is steadfast,*

*because we know that as you are par-
takers of the sufferings, so also you will
partake of the consolation.*

Notice that the source of comfort is God; but notice also God uses us to extend that comfort. God allows troubles to enter our lives so that we, being comforted, may pass God's comfort on.

Often we are like Jesus' disciples in the boat while the storm rages. Like them we cry, "Lord, don't You care? We are perishing. Death stares us in the face." And Jesus simply says to the wind and the waves, "Peace be still." At once upon the sea and in the sky there is a great calm. In times like that, Jesus wonders why His friends don't believe in Him always. And so He adds, "Why don't you believe? You are of little faith."

As long as the Creator God of all the universe is in the same boat with us, why do we let ourselves become so terrified, O we of little faith? Let us receive and pass along what we have received from the well of every blessing (to mix a few metaphors).

> *"If I really trust Him*
> *Shall I ever fret?*
> *If I really do expect Him*
> *Can I e'er forget?*

If by faith I really see Him
Shall I doubt His aid?
If I really, really love Him
Can I be afraid?"

—ANONYMOUS

We want to love You more, Lord. Help us to love each other more as well.

12

DARE TO LOVE

Beloved, let us love one another,
for love is of God;
and everyone who loves is
born of God and knows God.
1 JOHN 4:7

We serve an audacious God. That word audacious as a description of God is challenging but true. The word means "reckless daring." Often God trusts us more than seems reasonable.

God trusted the whole future of human existence to the hands of a young Jewish girl named Mary. Knowing all the frailties of humanity and human bodies, God allowed His Son to be born like each of us and to be brought up by a young girl. In the same way, God trusts those who are willing to put their trust in Him. And God uses them to do the impossible.

If you were creating the earthly body of Christ, the Church, would you have left it in the hands of that small group of Jesus' disciples? We probably wouldn't have dared, but God did—and here we are, the Church, the body of Christ! We need to remember one fact: "With God all things are possible." Another fact to remember is His power and strength are at their greatest when we realize how little we have.

What I'm trying to say is that it is impossible to fail in bringing comfort to others. Whatever we do, so long as we act in love, God will use. But we need to be more daring in our reaching out to those in need of comfort and help. We have become a people afraid to make commitments; we step back, we turn away, we stay safe. I'm afraid we're all too much like the priest and the Levite who went on by the wounded traveler, keeping as far away as possible.

But Jesus calls us to be like the Samaritan who went out of his way to help the wounded traveler. Christ asks us to love those who are threatened by life's storms. We, too, need to be audacious in our love.

COMFORT FOR THOSE WHO GRIEVE

Strong Son of God, immortal Love,
Whom we, that have not seen Thy face,
By faith, and faith alone, embrace,
Believing where we cannot prove.

Thou seemest human and divine,
The highest, holiest manhood, Thou:
Our wills are ours, we know not
how—
Our wills are ours, to make them Thine.
—ALFRED TENNYSON

Make us audacious for You, Lord.

13

A Sweet Aroma

Ointment and perfume delight the heart,
And the sweetness of a man's friend
gives delight by hearty counsel.
PROVERBS 27:9

It is so easy to thoughtlessly add to others' hurt in their time of grief. Always what we say or what we do must be governed by the restraint and thoughtfulness of love. Job had his comforters who were so busy defending their philosophies that they could not comfort. And often we run into friends and loved ones who offer us "comfort" that only wounds us more. At the time of our son's death, one woman informed my wife that Philip's death was God's way of controlling the population explosion. My wife felt deeply hurt.

My wife's aunt Mary lost her husband of sixty-plus years. They had not been able to have children, so after his death, she had no one close for support; she was left to suffer her grief alone. Aunt Mary missed her husband greatly. About a month after his death, while buying groceries, she overheard two women discussing her. One said to the other, "I don't know why Mary feels so bad still. After all, Ernest has been gone for a month now." I'm sure those women had never experienced the awfulness of being left to face life alone. Many years have passed since this incident, and I wonder now if they can speak more lovingly and with more understanding as they, too, have become acquainted with grief.

Of course, there will always be someone who does not understand. Jesus ran into people like that, too. There was that time when Jesus' friend Mary took a very costly perfumed oil and poured it out to anoint His feet. Further humbling herself, she used her long hair to wipe His feet. As a result, the aroma of that act of worship has perfumed the centuries. She comforted Christ by giving her flowers of appreciation and love before His death. But there was at least one who was scandalized by such a waste. Judas was affronted—but Jesus reminded him gently that Mary's act of love looked forward to a time when He, Christ, would die.

No act of love given in our Savior's name is ever unrewarded. In Romans 12:1, Paul writes, "I beseech you therefore, brethren, by the mercies of God, that you present your bodies a living sacrifice, holy, acceptable to God, which is your reasonable service." Let your life give off the sweet aroma of consolation to those who hurt.

> *Little deeds of kindness*
> *Little words of love*
> *Help to make earth happy*
> *Like the heaven above.*
> —JULIA A. CARNEY

May all our words, Lord, be scented with Your love.

14

SIMPLE ACTS OF LOVE

With goodwill doing service,
as to the Lord,
and not to men.
EPHESIANS 6:7

Sometimes as we struggle with everyday life, the rest of life seems to pass us by; we haven't time to be a great worker for God. Our hearts are willing to do great things for God; we long to be a part of His great chain of love and comfort. But the reality of our lives is that we're just so busy with the daily responsibilities of family and home that we don't have much time left over.

The truth is, though, even something as simple as washing dishes and getting meals can be used by God. And remember, God does not call us all to mission fields in foreign lands. For most of us, God's first call is to those who are closest to us, the ones with whom we share our homes, our neighbors, and our friends. Sometimes those near and dear ones are so close that we almost forget about them. But they are the very ones with whom we can share God's comfort in the most constant and tangible ways.

Brother Lawrence, a medieval monk, found the joy of practicing the presence of God in every task, no matter how small or ordinary. How great is the reward to people like this who simply give of themselves in the midst of the trials and encumbrances of their own lives!

Did not Christ promise that even a cup of water given in His name is noticed by the Father and has its reward? May God bless all of you who care enough to sacrifice time and strength to be a comfort to others.

We cannot escape our responsibility to comfort others. We cannot escape by pleading inability or lack of time. When we act with little strength, then God is able to accomplish the most. When we had so little to offer, God gave Himself for us. In the midst of our uselessness, God gave love.

Lord of all pots and pans and things,
*   since I've no time to be*
A saint by doing lovely things, or
*   watching late with Thee,*
Or dreaming in the dawn-light, or
*   storming Heaven's gates,*
Make me a saint by getting meals and
*   washing up the plates.*

Warm all the kitchen with Thy love, and
*   light it with Thy peace;*
Forgive me all my worryings, and make
*   my grumbling cease.*
Thou who didst love to give men food
*   in room or by the sea,*
Accept this service that I do—
*   I do it unto Thee.*
*   —CECILY HALLECK*

Use us, Lord. We want even our smallest, most ordi-
nary acts to spread Your comfort.

PART IV

VICTORY IN
THE MIDST OF AFFLICTION

We have discussed the comfort that God offers us, the comfort that He asks us to pass on to others. But the trials we face are so intense, and we are so very weak. How can we find the strength to even reach out to God for the comfort He offers, let alone find the courage to pass it on to those around us? In ourselves, we will never find victory in the midst of our terrible affliction. Can God somehow protect us from our lives' fiery trials. . . ?

1

WE ARE LOVED

"For God so loved the world that
He gave His only begotten Son,
that whoever believes in Him
should not perish
but have everlasting life."
JOHN 3:16

I don't understand why trials and tribulation, grief and sorrow seek to kill our souls. Nor do I understand how Christ brings us out of our sorrow by the power of His comfort and healing. All I know is that He does. He knows the way, for He has already walked the same rough path we are traveling now. "Man of sorrows and acquainted with grief," is the prophet Isaiah's description of Him. "Surely He has borne our griefs and carried our sorrows" (Isaiah 53:3–4). He knows the darkness that falls upon us—and He cares for us.

> *But He was wounded for our transgressions, He was bruised for our iniquities; the chastisement for our peace was upon Him, and by His stripes we are healed. All we like sheep have gone astray; we have turned, every one, to his own way; and the LORD has laid on Him the iniquity of us all.*
> ISAIAH 53:5–6

When sin separates us from God, when we stand alone rejected, when grief overpowers us, God has a way of escape—a path is put before each of us, purchased by the sacrifice of His own Son, because we are loved with an unconditional love. His comfort and peace are ours. Push away the doubts and simply accept by faith that God loves us.

Probably of all the verses I have learned, the first, John 3:16, is the most important to me. It still stands as a bulwark, a foundation, a resting place. It is my very assurance and hope in my walk through life: God so loved the world that He gave His Son.

When the troubles "like sea billows roll,"

seeking to overwhelm us, when grief tears at the very fabric of our being and the darkness of our souls clouds the light of His presence, we have hope as a bright leading star, and we know with confidence and comfort that He cares. We can come boldly to His throne of grace and mercy. He hears and He will answer our prayers. He loves us.

> *Thro' the love of God, our Saviour,*
>   *All will be well;*
> *Free and changeless is His favor,*
>   *All, all is well.*
> *Precious is the blood that healed us;*
>   *Perfect is the grace that sealed us;*
> *Strong the hand stretched out to shield us,*
>   *All must be well.*
>
> —MARY PETERS

Somehow, someway, we know, Lord, that all things are well because of You.

2

THE FIERY FURNACE
OF AFFLICTION

Do not rejoice over me, my enemy;
When I fall, I will arise;
When I sit in darkness,
The LORD will be a light to me.
MICAH 7:8

The Book of Daniel is an exciting book. Here we get glimpses into the future—and in that future we see God still in control. Looking back, we see that the children of Israel, the Jews, had been removed to a foreign land where they had forgotten their God. But in their captivity, God had not forgotten them. He was still the God of all comfort. He was very present with them in their problems and in their possibilities.

This Old Testament book gives us the account of the fiery furnace. In this story, three men made a choice for God—and God did not fail them in their awful time of need. He brought them comfort in the midst of fire and peril.

Shadrach, Meshach, and Abednego got into trouble with their captor-king when they refused to bow down and worship the great image he had erected. They were told very plainly, "If you do not worship, you shall be cast immediately into the midst of a burning fiery furnace. And who is the god who will deliver you from my hands?" (Daniel 3:15).

Shadrach, Meshach, and Abednego were not sure of the outcome—but they were sure of their God. They answered: "O Nebuchadnezzar, we have no need to answer you in this matter. If that is the case, our God whom we serve is able to deliver us from the burning fiery furnace, and He will deliver us from your hand, O king. But if not, let it be known to you, O king, that we do not serve your gods, nor will we worship the gold image which you have set up" (Daniel 3:16–18).

Now that statement really made the king angry. There are times when our choice can only be for God and nothing else—and we will encounter anger at our lack of compliance. But we can do no different than those three did, for like them, our hope is in the living God, the eternal God.

And so the king "blew his stack" and ordered a special reception for them: The furnace was made seven times hotter than ever before. The king was intent on making sure that they would be burned to a crisp! He would show those upstarts from Israel! They were bound and cast into the flames.

I've often wondered just what that furnace was like. Was it a brick kiln? We are not told, but we do know that the fire was so hot that it killed those who were ordered to throw the three men to the flames! So you can imagine the astonishment of the king when he saw those three men walk freely in the midst of the flames—and then he saw another walking with them. The king cried out, "Didn't we throw three into the fire? But I see four and that fourth One is like a Son of God."

Strange and mighty things happen when by faith we trust in God. God did not neglect the three Israelite men in their hour of need. He brought them the comfort of His protection and His presence. And He will not fail us either.

Too often we end up in the fiery furnaces of affliction, even though we have done no wrong.

Marriages crumble and our hearts break; we cannot stand the awful reality of failure in our profession or work; loved ones die; we watch all our hopes crumble. But there, in the midst of the fires of our anguish, we find Jesus. He restores purpose and meaning to our lives. He will be the God of all comfort to us.

He owns me for His child;
I can no longer fear.
With confidence I now draw nigh,
And, "Abba, Father," cry.
                                    —CHARLES WESLEY

Take all our fears away, Lord. Help us to know that even in the fiery furnace of affliction, You are with us.

3

LIGHT IN THE LION'S DEN

"These things I have spoken to you,
that in Me you may have peace.
In the world you will have tribulation;
but be of good cheer, I have overcome the world."
JOHN 16:33

The Book of Daniel tells us another story about comfort in the midst of trials. Remember Daniel in the lion's den?

Although he was kept by the certainty of God's presence, Daniel still spent a night in the lion's den. He escaped—but centuries later thousands of Christians fell prey to the hungry lions of the Roman coliseums. We can't help but ask, Why was Daniel spared and not those faithful believers in Christ? Obviously, God does not always choose to save Christians from tragedy and death.

The apostle Paul knew the suffering of living for Christ—but until Paul's work was done, God kept him safe even in the midst of pain and trials. I used to think that Christians were not subject to the terrors and storms of this world, but I know differently now—just as I am also absolutely certain that God is still faithful to His own in every fiery furnace and frightening lion's den.

When, in spite of everything, you are caught in a situation that has no exits, stand true to God. Walk with Him into the furnace. Go unafraid into the portal that seems to lead to destruction. There in the darkness of the lion's den He will deliver you from the jaws of the adversary. With your loving Heavenly Father's touch of comfort, you, too, can walk courageously the ways of sickness, death, and sorrow. Crushed by defeat after defeat, broken by unrealized hopes, you, too, can walk through it all with victory. Don't just take my word for it. That is exactly what God says!

Yet I will be honest with you. It isn't always easy. It can be terrifying. Hang on. Look for the dawn of God's help and presence. Never forget the assurance of Psalm 30:5: "His favor is for life; weeping may endure for a night, but joy comes in the morning."

The Dawn of Hope

I fear no foe, with Thee at hand to bless;
Ills have no weight, and tears no
　　bitterness.
Where is death's sting? where, grave, thy
　　victory?
I triumph still, if Thou abide with me.
Hold Thou Thy cross before my closing eyes;
Shine through the gloom and point me to
　　the skies;
Heaven's morning breaks, and earth's vain
　　shadows flee;
In life, in death, O Lord, abide with me.
　　　　　　　　　—HENRY F. LYTE

Abide with us, Lord. Keep us safe in the midst of
danger. Help us to wait for the morning's joy.

4

CANDLES
IN THE DARKNESS

For You will light my lamp;
The LORD my God will
enlighten my darkness.
PSALM 18:28

The twentieth century has come to its end. It has been a century of progress beyond our wildest dreams. In my more than eighty years of life, I have seen the Model T and the so-called luxury autos of those days turn into the dependable and comfortable cars we take for granted today. The rattly early airplanes became the giants in which we travel to the far corners of the earth. The radio, followed by television, has brought the world into our homes. With the electrification of America, light shines all around us. The old washboard and washtubs have been replaced with our modern washers and dryers. (But despite all the "necessary" appliances and conveniences of today, we manage to live just as busy—or busier—lives than ever.) The computer has gone where no one had ever gone before. This century has seen great progress in the field of medicine—and yet cancer is still with us, and AIDS fills our hearts with terror.

In the twentieth century, untold millions of our brothers and sisters in Christ perished in the fiery furnaces of prejudice and hate because of their faith. The killing fields of China, Russia, Cambodia, Africa, South America (to name only a few) are saturated with the blood of these martyrs.

In this world of senseless war, many mothers helplessly watch their children die of hunger and disease. How hard it must be! Our hearts are torn when on TV we see the children's pitiful emaciated bodies, flies buzzing around their faces. Does God see? Certainly He sees! Not even a sparrow falls but He sees. My only comfort is the knowledge that He has something far better prepared for all who suffer.

We face the new century with fear. Our need for God is great. We need His touch on our lives, our families, our government, and our world. Is the end of all things at hand? I cannot say, but without a doubt we do live in perilous times.

But God was in the furnace with those three Israelite men. He was in the lion's den with Daniel. And the Lord will be in the midst of the multitudes who give their lives for Him. What is more, He has promised to be with you wherever you may be. Look for His touch of comfort when you, too, suffer. It is real. It will comfort and heal.

And yet we each need to pray, "Father, is there more I can do? Can I rest when You have done so much for me? Show me my part in bringing comfort to the world. Use me to bring Your light to our dark world."

A charge to keep I have,
A God to glorify,
A never dying soul to save,
And fit it for the skies.

To serve the present age,
My calling to fulfill;
O may it all my powers engage
To do my Master's will!

THE DAWN OF HOPE

Help me to watch and pray,
And still on Thee rely,
O let me not my trust betray,
But press to realms on high.
                                   —CHARLES WESLEY

Help us, Lord, to be candles in the darkness.

5

KEEPING THE FAITH

*I have fought the good fight,
I have finished the race, I have kept the faith.
Finally, there is laid up for me
the crown of righteousness,
which the Lord, the righteous Judge,
will give to me on that Day,
and not to me only but also to all
who have loved His appearing.*
2 TIMOTHY 4:7–8

My wife and I first met Ruth Wager when we went to the tuberculosis hospital at a friend's request, believing God would want us to give comfort to this sick woman. How wrong we were! Ruth asked no comfort from us; instead, her only concern was giving God's love and joy to others. We left wondering why we had ever complained about anything in our lives.

Unable to write, she composed poetry in her mind, which others wrote down for her. I have included many of her poems in this book, because I have found her words continue to speak to me down through the years; I hope they will speak to your hearts as well. When I first met Ruth, a line in one of her many poems struck me forcefully: "I am not sick! It is my body that's sick." And how true that was!

Ruth was about twenty when tuberculosis attacked her. At the same time, the young man she was about to marry suddenly died. Then her brother with whom she was very close was killed in an accident. Her whole world crashed about her. And it was then God strengthened her faith with His comforting presence. That Presence supported her with love and joy.

When we walked in the room, not knowing what to expect, we were greeted with a huge smile on the face of a young woman nearly thirty. She had once been a beautiful girl, but now she was wasted away to the point of skin and bones. She talked animatedly of her life in the hospital, finding humor even in the painful treatments. But always the conversation came back to her Lord. Her life radiated her love for Him who had died for her.

In the last stages of tuberculosis, Ruth was very weak and confined to her bed. She had just strength enough to push a button that projected a page of a book on the ceiling so she could read. She had a tentlike frame over her, since she could not bear the weight of bedcovers. Her voice was very weak but always cheerful.

We called on her many times. Each time we left exalted, lifted up by the strength of her joy and faith. Her health worsened and we saw her for the last time just a week before the Lord called her home. That last visit was a time of triumphant victory, even though she was so very weak. Her voice was but a faint whisper. Smiling seemed to take all her strength, but her lips twitched with a ghost of the smile we had come to love.

What joy must have been hers when, entirely whole in heaven's home, she heard her Savior say, "Well done, thou good and faithful servant, enter into your rest."

We learned much from Ruth. No matter what life brings, the joy of the Lord can carry us through. She stood the test of her fiery furnace. With the help of the Lord, the lion's jaws did not devour her. With the apostle Paul, she could say with assurance: "I have fought the good fight."

THE DAWN OF HOPE

The day is done, the sun has set,
Yet light still tints the sky;
My heart stands still in reverence,
For God is passing by.

When life is done for me, O Lord,
One thing I'd like to know—
That I have made mine bright enough
To leave an afterglow.
—RUTH ALLA WAGER

Help us, Lord, to fight the good fight. When we are
gone, may our lives leave an afterglow.

6

THE FAITH OF JOB

"For I know that my Redeemer lives,
And He shall stand at last on the earth."
JOB 19:25

Have you ever heard the phrase "Job's troubles"? Job had them, and in one degree or another we all have them. Every time I sit watching the fire in our fireplace on a cold wintry night, I am reminded of Job's words: "Man is born to trouble, As the sparks fly upward" (5:7). I'm glad he didn't stop there. The words that follow give us the secret of comfort: "But as for me, I would seek God, and to God I would commit my cause."

In your darkest hour, think of Job and remember that Job kept his hope when all was utterly hopeless. With his body filled with infection and pain, he still hoped and believed in a purpose and a plan; he never doubted that his God understood and cared. But he had lost everything: His children were dead; his property and wealth had disappeared; his wife failed him when she didn't understand; he had friends but they came with empty comfort; and even God seemed so very far away in his awful time of trial and need. No wonder he cried out for a "daysman" (9:33 KJV), one who could come and truly understand his problem and his hurt. He desperately needed a Comforter who understood and cared, Someone who could stand between him and his great need.

But Job held onto one fact, no matter how buffeted he was by his pain and grief: He knew his God would never change. Job could have given up and believed that God had abandoned him—but he was held firm by faith. So in spite of everything, he was able to say with total acceptance:

> *"Naked I came from my mother's womb,*
> *and naked shall I return there. The LORD*
> *gave, and the LORD has taken away;*
> *blessed be the name of the LORD."*
>
> JOB 1:21

Job knew the nature of God and that knowledge kept him secure even in the midst of loss.

But when we are young in the faith, trials can deeply disturb our faith. In 1940, I was a student at Houghton College when Dan Engle, a senior and the designated valedictorian of his class, died suddenly from a strep infection. His future had been bright, but in the days before the common use of antibiotics, a slight cut from his razor killed him. The students and faculty, including myself, were hit hard. If God would allow Dan's death, could I really trust Him? But then in chapel we listened to a telegram from a missionary in Africa. The message read, "The Lord gave, and the Lord has taken away; blessed be the name of the Lord" —Job's words and Job's acceptance. Those words touched me. They stabilized my wavering faith.

Remember this: Though our faith wavers, God doesn't. In the words of Romans 8, "If God is for us, who can be against us?"

Through many dangers, toils, and snares.
I have already come;
'Tis grace hath brought me safe thus far,
And grace will lead me home.

THE DAWN OF HOPE

The Lord has promised good to me,
His Word my hope secures;
He will my shield and portion be
As long as life endures.
                    —JOHN NEWTON

When we waver, Lord, thank You that You stay firm.

7

HOPE

Therefore we also, since we are surrounded by
so great a cloud of witnesses [who have
experienced that fulfilled hope and glory],
let us lay aside every weight,
and the sin which so easily ensnares us,
and let us run with endurance the race
that is set before us, looking unto Jesus,
the author and finisher of our faith,
who for the joy that was set before Him
endured the cross, despising the shame,
and has sat down at the
right hand of the throne of God.
HEBREWS 12:1–2

Have you ever been tempted, when troubles come, to feel all alone, isolated in the midst of your dilemma? That's when we need Job's rock-solid assurance that ahead there is always a future—a future beyond the troubles, given to us by our loving Heavenly Father. With that future comes hope. And in the days of our trouble, that hope allows us to come to God, look up in His face, and declare, "I love You, Father, for You love me." Then we will be surprised by His peace and love.

It sounds so simple, and I wish it were. Too often, though, our woe looms larger than our vision. I have found, however, that the light of God's presence will break through the darkest of our nights in His time and in His way. I do not quite understand the promise of Psalm 30, verse 5: "Weeping may endure for a night, but joy comes in the morning." And to make it more disturbing, the original language says, "But a shout of joy comes in the morning." How can we shout for joy when we have lost those whom we love the most? And yet somehow, someway, God will not only ease our pain but replace it with a joy so bright and exuberant that we'll want to shout. But how very long some of our nights are—sleepless, restless, without comfort.

And yet these nights bring us to a wonderful reality. Beyond the dark clouds, God's hope shines like the sun. The same hope took Jesus from heaven's indescribable glory to the filth of earth's dark stable; from the infinite freedom and power of being God over all to the encumbrance of weak human flesh; from life to Calvary's cross; from death's dark tomb to the eternal light of resurrection's glory.

That hope allows us to pray, "Heavenly Father, God of all mercies and comfort, in the midst of this awfulness that has come to me, I am certain that You are here and that You really care about me. Hold me close, Lord. Let me feel Your great love. Help me to know without question that even this trial has come through the permissive grace of Your love for me. Help me to know that You care when I feel so alone and so blinded by the darkness of my grief. As I ran to my parents, I now run to You, Lord. I don't understand, but I trust You to make it better. May I feel Your touch. Hold me steady. Reassure me. Give me Your comfort. Let me experience the kiss of Your healing love. Amen."

I see Thy mercy, limitless as space,
I see Thy love and feel Thy close embrace;
And though Thy presence fills the universe,
Yet close as hands and heart Thou art to me.
                                    —Olga J. Weiss

Please, Lord, hug our hearts with Your hope.

PART V

THE SHEPHERD'S PSALM

He will feed His flock like a shepherd;
He will gather the lambs with His arm.
ISAIAH 40:11

Most of us are well acquainted with Psalm 23. There is hardly a funeral in which it is not quoted. Many are the times I have sought to bring comfort by reading it to those broken with grief and despair.

Yet its words hold truth that helps us face life as well as death. It speaks as clearly in our bright happy days as it does in the darkness of our nights. It gives us strength to meet the adversities of life, but it should be a deep source of joy at all times. In this part of this book, I want to take you into the fold of God's love as it is revealed here in this psalm. So come with me and meet the Shepherd. . . .

The LORD is my shepherd;
I shall not want.
He makes me to lie down in green
pastures;
He leads me beside the still waters.
He restores my soul;
He leads me in the paths of righteousness
For His name's sake.
Yea, though I walk through the valley of
the shadow of death,
I will fear no evil;
For You are with me;
Your rod and Your staff, they comfort me.
You prepare a table before me in the
presence of my enemies;
You anoint my head with oil;
My cup runs over.
Surely goodness and mercy shall follow me
All the days of my life;
And I will dwell in the house of the LORD
Forever.

PSALM 23

1

THE PERSON
OF THE SHEPHERD

But He was wounded [pierced through]
for our transgressions,
He was bruised for our iniquities;
The chastisement for our peace was upon Him,
and by His stripes we are healed.
ISAIAH 53:5

Especially in Oriental lands, the shepherd is very important to the welfare of the flock entrusted to him. Like it or not, the Bible likens us to sheep. . .for we, too, need Someone to care for us. Our Lord understood this about us, as we read in Matthew 9:36:

But when He saw the multitudes, He was moved with compassion for them, because they were weary and scattered, like sheep having no shepherd.

We, too, have been so utterly weary, so terribly confused, so lost in our problems. But we can find our Shepherd in Christ. He is my Shepherd. He is your Shepherd. He is our Shepherd. He is the Lord. Jehovah is His name. Yet He has chosen to identify Himself with us and our need.

Ever since I was a child, I have loved the message of the painting that portrays Christ, the Good Shepherd, reaching over the abyss to rescue His wandering sheep. From that painting, I learned how much my Savior cared for me. I was lost—and He sought me. "The LORD is my shepherd." We can place our life, our loves, our hopes, and our dreams into His hands without fear. And when life threatens to overwhelm us, He is there to lift us from our dilemmas.

Our Shepherd cares about each and every one of us in all our needs. The Lord is our Shepherd; we shall not want. He is the God of all comfort.

There were ninety and nine that safely lay
In the shelter of the fold,
But one was out on the hills away,

COMFORT FOR THOSE WHO GRIEVE

Far off from the gates of gold—
Away on the mountains wild and bare,
Away from the tender Shepherd's care.

"Lord, Thou hast here Thy ninety and nine;
Are they not enough for Thee?"
But the Shepherd made answer: "This of Mine
Has wandered away from Me;
And although the road be rough and steep
I go to the desert to find My sheep."

"Lord, whence are these blood drops all the way
That mark the mountain track?"
"They were shed for one who had gone astray
Ere the Shepherd could bring him back."—
"Lord, whence are Thy hands so rent and torn?"
"They are pierced tonight by many a thorn."

But all through the mountains, thunder riven,
And up from the rocky steep
There arose a glad cry to the gate of heaven,
"Rejoice! I have found my sheep!"
And the angels echoed around the Throne,
"Rejoice, for the Lord brings back His own!"
         —ELIZABETH CLEPHANE

Oh, Lord, our Shepherd, thank You for finding us
when we are lost.

2

THE PROVISION
OF THE SHEPHERD

"I am the good shepherd;
and I know My sheep,
and am known by My own."
JOHN 10:14

The Shepherd is sensitive to the needs of the sheep. He knows their limitations and that which will bring full satisfaction. We are the sheep of His pasture—and He identifies with us. He has lived our lives. Knowing our penalty of death and knowing the burden of our sins, He became the sacrificial Lamb, slain in our place that we might have eternal hope.

Not being an actual sheep, I can't quite envision the satisfaction of resting in a place where there are no cares, those "green pastures" of which Psalm 23 speaks. But I have to admit that there have been many times I have received refreshment that only God could give. Those were the times I took His advice to draw apart with Him. Those were the times I found the fountains of living water. I have heard that sheep have difficulty drinking where the current is swift and rough—and I know that in a similar way I need to shut out the hurry and tumult of life. When we pray, Christ advises us to close the door that separates us from "life out there."

During World War II, I spent almost six months in a defense plant, working on the wings of the old P40 fighter planes. I was amazed to find that during the lunch break, in the cafeteria with hundreds all about me, I could be alone with God. There, sitting at a table filled with talking, laughing diners, I was able to read my New Testament and pray and even prepare my Sunday sermons. I suppose some people must have thought I was a little strange, but no one objected. And if they did, I was not conscious of it. I shut the "door"! God restored my soul to face the work conditions and my own ineptitude. The Lord gave me miraculous skill in riveting, beyond my training and ability.

Another miracle happened the day I quit to

take my new church in Black Creek, New York, shortly before my marriage. The supervisor over several thousand came to see me—and among other things, he assured me that if he ever was in Black Creek on a Sunday, he was going to hear me preach. He never came, but I am still mystified why he came to see me at all, a lowly riveter. But for the Lord's name's sake, "He led me in the paths of righteousness."

It is exciting to experience the leading of the Lord. I have watched lives being changed, including mine. Looking back over eighty-two years, I can truthfully say that His way has been a rich and glorious way. Even in the loss of our son, He was there to bring light into the awfulness of the shadows. Good came from even that terrible tragedy.

I have had a good life with a wonderful wife and family. And now the Dawn of eternity draws even closer as I grow older. Until the Dawn, I plan to follow where He leads. Life is sure exciting when we walk with the Shepherd!

> *He leadeth me; O blessed thought!*
> *O words with heavenly comfort fraught!*
> *Whatever I do, wherever I be,*
> *Still 'tis God's hand that leadeth me.*

He leadeth me, He leadeth me,
By His own hand He leadeth me:
His faithful follower I would be,
For by His hand He leadeth me.
                              —JOSEPH GILMORE

Thank You, Lord, for leading us.

3

THE PROTECTION
OF THE SHEPHERD

*Yea, though I walk through the valley
of the shadow of death,
I will fear no evil;
For You are with me;
Your rod and Your staff,
they comfort me.*
PSALM 23:4

How comforting are these words. In this book
we have talked of death and dying, of sorrow and
grief, of hurt and loneliness. But we also have
talked of the comfort and the strength that the
Lord alone is able to impart to us in the nights
of our trouble. We have the assurance of the
Dawn—and in the meantime, we know that we

do not walk alone through the dark valley of death's shadow. God walks with us all the way.

We do not have to wait for eternity's Dawn; we have the assurance of God's presence right now on this old earth in every circumstance in which we find ourselves. When in our desperation we realize how much we need Him, we will always sense His loving presence. I'm beginning to realize how much time is spent in worry and anticipation, when we should be shouting for joy that our Shepherd is leading us into the glories of the eternal Dawn!

I have gone on tours of limestone caves where the guide suddenly extinguished all the lights. How dark was that darkness! When our lives are touched by tragedy and grief, we, too, feel as though we have been plunged into absolute blackness, a darkness that holds no light of any kind. But if we listen, we will hear the Shepherd comfort us that this dark valley is but a shadow of death. Because of Christ, we will never have to face absolute night, for on the cross He plunged Himself into the total darkness of death that we might only experience death's shadow. That shadow is deep and dark enough to chill our hearts—but our Shepherd will never leave us. His "rod and staff" will comfort us.

Edward Anderson was one of the great evangelists we were privileged to have in our churches over the years. When he visited the Holy Land, he told us, the part he enjoyed most was the time he spent with the shepherds on Bethlehem's hills. There the Twenty-third Psalm became alive to him, and at least once in each evangelistic meeting he brought that psalm alive to his listeners.

He told of a narrow, deep ravine through which the shepherds lead their flocks, seeking green pastures. The way was in deep shadow; it wound around through rocks that hid the shepherd from the sheep's view; but without hesitation they followed after him. Although they could not see him, they knew his presence was there as they followed the sound of his rod and staff striking the rocks along the dark way.

Reverend Anderson told of the times he watched the shepherds gather outside the sheepfold in the morning to go into the fields with their sheep. At each shepherd's distinctive call, his own flock would separate themselves from the other sheep and follow him to pasture. Reverend Anderson practiced one of those calls until he was sure he could call it exactly as the shepherd did. The next morning the shepherds gathered around him to see him call the sheep. He thought his call was perfect, but the sheep didn't even raise their heads. They weren't fooled.

And Christ's sheep also know His voice! When you find yourself in the valley of shadow, listen to the sounds of His rod and staff in the clatter of casseroles and cakes brought to your door by caring neighbors. Feel His gentle touch in those loving hugs, those silent pats on the back when words fail, those acts of love and caring, and especially the prayers of support. In all these we know His presence. He leads through life—and as the shadows lengthen toward our night, we know we will hear His rod and staff lead us home.

> *Ten thousand times ten thousand*
> *In sparkling raiment bright,*
> *The armies of the ransomed saints*
> *Throng up the steps of light;*
> *'Tis finished, all is finished,*
> *Their fight with death and sin;*
> *So let the victors in!*
>
> —HENRY ALFORD

Help us to hear the sound of Your rod and staff, Lord.
Lead us through both life and death.

4

THE PREPARATION
OF THE SHEPHERD

*You prepare a table before me
in the presence of my enemies;
You anoint my head with oil;
My cup runs over.*
PSALM 23:5

Our Lord definitely has a sense of humor. Or perhaps He demonstrates justice in action. Notice these next words: "You prepare a table before me in the presence of my enemies." There is the enemy, ignorant of his own starving condition, shut out, standing outside the circle of God's holy presence. He is forced to look on while those he sought to destroy are pampered by a loving God who prepares a feast beyond imagining.

The enemy is defeated! We know victory! We know the outpouring of God's infinite, unconditional love. And soon we will come to that Day that is soon to dawn:

> *"Let us be glad and rejoice and give Him glory, for the marriage of the Lamb has come, and His wife [the Church] has made herself ready."*
>
> REVELATION 19:7

We've got an invitation. The Shepherd has prepared a great marriage feast for each one of us. It is sure going to be wonderful to see Jesus! And I hope I get a chance to see and greet each of you. We will sit down together at the table He has prepared for us. We will forget all about the darkness that shadowed our lives.

No more sorrows! No more tears! All because Jesus was willing to take the cup of Gethsemane, the cup of obedience, and drink it for us. On that awful day on Calvary, God the Son gave Himself to die on the cross in your place and in mine. This is the way He prepared the table to which He will welcome us in heaven. When I think of what He did, my cup runs over with thanksgiving, praise, and joy!

But you can't come to the Lord's marriage

table if you are still clinging to your old life, with all its destructive habits. "Come and eat!" Jesus calls us. "Lay down your rusty weapons. Put aside your bitterness and anger. There is plenty here for you. Come and share My joy and peace forever."

> *Make me a captive, Lord,*
> *And then I shall be free;*
> *Force me to render up my sword*
> *And I shall conqueror be,*
> *I sink in life's alarms*
> *When by myself I stand;*
> *Imprison me within Thine arms,*
> *And strong shall be my hand.*
>
> —UNKNOWN

Thank You, Lord, for preparing the table for us. Help us to lay down all our weapons, and join You at the Lamb's marriage feast.

5

THE PROMISE
OF THE SHEPHERD

Surely goodness and mercy shall follow me
All the days of my life.
PSALM 23:6

Someone once called goodness and mercy the two sheepdogs of the Shepherd; they are the things that guide us into the fold. Because Christ is good and because He is merciful, He has gathered us into His safety.

I like watching a good sheepdog—or cow dog—do his job. He knows what is expected of him, and he does it well and faithfully. Swinging wide, he turns the whole flock at the shepherd's command. Going in front, sometimes even running across the backs of the flock to get there, he brings the flock to a halt. He even separates individual sheep from the flock. In the same way, the sheepdogs of our Shepherd work well at His command.

The darkness of night is upon us! The times of loneliness beset our souls! Now is when we need the comforting of the Good Shepherd:

> *I would have lost heart, unless I had believed*
> *That I would see the goodness of the Lord*
> *In the land of the living.*
>
> PSALM 27:13

We don't have to wait for heaven to be comforted; God's comfort is for right now. Right now in the present moment, our Heavenly Father provides that comfort. He provides it because He is good and He is merciful; that is His promise to us. He knows our great need now!

All this is assured to us. He has made His promise, and our Father does not lie. We can claim this promise if we reverence and accept Him as He is: Creator God, Unconditional Love, Lord of Lords, and King of Kings!

We are all partakers of human nature. I am glad to know that our Father's will is that we should partake of His nature as well. We grieve.

We weep. Our sorrow is great in our loneliness. We are hurt. Life has not been good or fair. And yet His mercy and goodness will be with us now —and one day we will greet the Dawn.

The God who brings us comfort meets us now in our need. That is part of His promise to us; but we have an even greater promise as well: He will meet us in the heavens when this life is past and we shall be in Him complete. Peace at last! Victory forever over the storms of life.

But until the Dawn, we still need the comfort of His abiding presence. Until the Dawn, we wait, finding in our Shepherd strength for our days and comfort for our sorrows. But in that great Day of resurrection and eternity we shall meet Him face-to-face and. . .

"And God will wipe away every tear from their eyes; there shall be no more death, nor sorrow, nor crying. There shall be no more pain, for the former things have passed away."

REVELATION 21:4

Unconditional Love, Lord of Lords, thank You that You promise us life and joy forever.

PART VI

THE LIGHT OF DAWN

Now as we come to the end of this book, I want to focus for a little while on that word I have referred to so often: the Dawn. When I have spoken of "dawn" throughout these pages, I have been referring to two related concepts: first, "the dawn of comfort," the time when our dark night of grief and sorrow will end and we will again see the light. That emotional dawn is only a reflection of the other Dawn of which I've spoken, the great morning of eternity when all death shall end forever and we shall see our Savior's face. . . .

1

Joy in the Morning

We are hard pressed on every side, yet not crushed;
we are perplexed, but not in despair;
persecuted, but not forsaken;
struck down, but not destroyed.
Therefore we do not lose heart.
Even though our outward man is perishing,
yet the inward man is being renewed day by day.
2 Corinthians 4:8–9, 16

At some time or other grief will come upon each of us. But equally certain is the fact that God will not leave us in the darkness of our grief. Our acquaintance with grief will never be pleasant: Our bodies may become weakened and succumb to disease; our minds may be subjected to the depression and darkness of hopelessness; our spirits may experience the insecurity of doubt and despair. Yet God's morning will dawn for us if we trust Him. We who questioned our ability to survive the storm will be enabled to survive and see God's faithfulness and love.

The psalmist promised, "Weeping may endure for a night, but joy comes in the morning" (Psalm 30:5). And yet I'm sure that some of you are asking, "Why does the night last so very long?" I remember a father who had lost a child asking me, "Does it ever stop hurting? Does it ever get better?"

I know that nothing is so destructive as the darkness of the soul—but I also know that dawn will come if we open our eyes and let God bring us out of the darkness as He parts the clouds of grief's night. I've been there. The dawn finally came. It broke slowly, but the wonder of His peace continues to this day.

I saw that dawn because I have a Heavenly Father who not only saw my need, but He saw the need of all humanity through all ages, and He sent His Son, Jesus, as a Man of Sorrows and acquainted with grief. Christ's death on the cross assures us that the dawn will come. I cannot say what heaven will be like, but I know that there is no night there—no death, no grief, no tears. That is the dawn we will all have in Jesus, not only for now, but for eternity.

Have you ever thought about what dawn really means? Dawn—a new light, a new day, a new hope, an opportunity to begin anew. Dawn brings a quickening of our spirits, and it gives us a new song in our hearts.

Dawn is a gift given to us that we might see in it the face of God. It is a time to acknowledge His presence and power in the glory of His creation. It is a time to revel in the pageantry and color of creation. At dawn God opens His hand, glory shines forth, and eternal light dispels night. A new day is born.

> *Joyful, joyful, we adore Thee,*
> *God of Glory, Lord of love;*
> *Hearts unfold like flowers before Thee,*
> *Opening to the sun above.*
> *Melt the clouds of sin and sadness,*
> *Drive the dark of doubt away;*
> *Giver of immortal gladness,*
> *Fill us with the light of day.*
> —HENRY VAN DYKE

Dear Lord, give us joy in Your new day.

2

LIME LAKE, 1938

But if we walk in the light as He is in the light,
we have fellowship with one another,
and the blood of Jesus Christ His Son
cleanses us from all sin.
1 JOHN 1:7

I will never forget one long-ago dawn in 1938 when I was twenty-one years old. I was a new Christian, and that summer our pastor took a group of young people to the Odasagih Bible Conference at Lime Lake in western New York State. I was working, so on the weekend a friend and I hitchhiked up to join them.

Since there was no room for us in the cabins, we improvised a bed in a rented rowboat. Being rocked by the lake's gentle waves was a great way to go to sleep; in fact, we slept exceptionally well. But I woke early, just as the sky began to brighten.

No clouds were in the sky and only a few stars lingered; all about me was a great hush. Mist hovered in tenuous strands over the calm waters of the lake. Even the dance hall that had so noisily proclaimed its presence the night before was quiet, asleep in the covering mist. Everywhere the mist softened the harsh intrusion of human presence. Except for the soft whisper of the gentle waves lapping against the boat and the occasional splash of a leaping fish, there was not a sound.

At that moment, on that calm lake with God and His creation, I could very easily imagine that I had stepped back to the beginning of time. I contemplated the words of Job, who spoke with wonder of that first dawn when the morning stars sang together. That morning at Lime Lake, I was humbled before God's presence and creation, while at the same time I exulted at being a part of His newness. His dawn was in my heart.

Then, in the distance, I heard the crowing of a rooster, the bark of a dog, a farmer calling his cows to the barn for milking. I began to hear voices, the sound of a car on the highway. The clouds were crimson and orange, on fire in the midst of a robin's egg blue sky. Then the sun burst forth in fiery radiance on a new day.

That morning brought a special glory to my heart; my soul was created anew, and all nature joined in the wonder of it all. So now when I speak of a new dawn after the dark night of grief, I remember the glory of that morning when God revealed Himself to me on Lime Lake. And I look forward to when the Dawn of eternal Day will burst upon us.

The sands of time are sinking,
The dawn of heaven breaks.
The summer morn I've longed for,
The fair sweet morn awakes.
Dark, dark has been the midnight,
But dayspring is at hand,
And glory, glory dwells in Immanuel's
land.

—ANN ROSE COUSINS

Shine the glory of Your sunrise in our hearts, dear Lord.

3

THE PROMISE OF THE DAWN

For now we see in a mirror,
dimly, but then face to face.
Now I know in part,
but then I shall know
just as I also am known.
1 CORINTHIANS 13:12

That morning on Lime Lake, my friend slept on. He never realized the sunrise he had missed. It's amazing how many dawns I, too, have missed because they weren't important enough or I slept through them. Or worst of all, I allowed the night to linger in my heart. How often we allow apprehension, unresolved worries, or lingering pain to rob us of the new day God promises to those who look to Him. However, no matter how cloudy my eyes may sometimes be, I cannot escape the fact—I have experienced the dawn. I am touched by His light.

All those glorious sunrises that God in His love has given this world will pale before the wondrous beauty and pageantry of that Day that will fulfill all the hopes and promises of the ages. We shall see our Lord face-to-face. In that Day, we will truly come out into the light. The sorrows and pains of this life will forever be forgotten; all the broken hearts shall be made whole. All the broken promises and all the lies shall be covered by His mercy and love. Loneliness will be replaced by God's loving presence. Then we shall know true fellowship with the Father, the Son, the Holy Spirit, and our brothers and sisters in the redeemed and sanctified church. Our great enemy, death, shall be no more.

God is interested in us and our need, and we don't need to wait until the door of death opens for us. God has a dawn for us right now, here in the midst of our lives, as He calls, "Come to Me, all you who labor and are heavy laden, and I will give you rest" (Matthew 11:28).

Here we still ask, "Why, Lord?"—and perhaps, "Why me?" We have no choice but to live by faith, unable to see the design of the tapestry He is weaving of our lives. But one day the

Dawn will truly come and we shall see the glory and the wonder of the sufferings of this life. But until then,

> *But if we hope for what we do not see, we eagerly wait for it with perseverance. Likewise the Spirit also helps in our weaknesses. For we do not know what we should pray for as we ought, but the Spirit Himself makes intercession for us with groanings which cannot be uttered. Now He who searches the hearts knows what the mind of the Spirit is, because He makes intercession for the saints according to the will of God. And we know that all things work together for good to those who love God, to those who are the called according to His purpose.*
>
> Romans 8:25–28

But you say, "What hope do I have? I'm not a saint!" Well, let me tell you, in God's eyes, a saint is one who has called on Him for mercy, been forgiven of sin, and is living in faith in the continuing grace of God. Anyone can be a saint. We must grasp God's Word as reality and live by faith in the completed work of Christ. He has purchased a sunrise even now for you and me. There can be joy in our mornings.

We expect a bright tomorrow;
All will be well;
Faith can sing thro' days of sorrow,
All, all is well.
On our Father's love relying,
Jesus ev'ry need supplying;
Or in living, or in dying,
All must be well.

—MARY PETERS

Help us, Lord, to wait for Your dawn. Renew us day by day.

4

Homecoming

He will swallow up death forever,
And the Lord GOD will wipe away
tears from all faces;
The rebuke of His people
He will take away from all the earth;
For the LORD has spoken.
ISAIAH 25:8

How I wish that no one had to go through grief's despair and darkness. But I know we must all face it, so we would do well to be prepared. Some people try to deny the reality of death, while others treat it as something to be feared; they live their lives under the shadow of that fear. But through Christ we are set free. Instead of fear, we have hope. Instead of an unknown, fearful future, we have the certainty of God's love and purpose, if by faith we reach out to Him.

Acquainted with grief, we fear, but we need not despair! With Christ, death no longer destroys but renews. Instead of darkness, before us is the dawn of a new Day that has no end, a day when God Himself ensures that we shall weep no more.

Death is real, too real now. It separates us from our loved ones, and one day it shall separate us from these bodies and these lives so dear to us. But sin is a defeated foe, vanquished by Christ's death on the cross and His resurrection from the dead.

No wonder we greet the Easter season with songs of praise and rejoicing. Jesus is risen! The chains of death are broken. We are free if we will but walk forth in the freedom of faith. There is set before us a great Homecoming and a great Reunion. Christ was a Man of Sorrows and acquainted with grief, so that we might become living examples of His grace and mercy. He is the One who gives songs in the night.

He is Lord Sabaoth—the Lord of all the hosts of heaven—the Almighty God. We can trust Him with our griefs, our burdens, and our sin, for He will bring us home.

COMFORT FOR THOSE WHO GRIEVE

A mighty fortress is our God,
A bulwark never failing;
Our helper He amid the flood
Of mortal ills prevailing.
For still our ancient foe
Doth seek to work us woe—
His craft and power are great,
And armed with cruel hate,
On earth is not his equal.

Did we in our own strength confide,
Our striving would be losing,
Were not the right Man on our side,
The Man of God's own choosing.
Dost ask who that may be?
Christ Jesus, it is He.
Lord Sabaoth His name,
From age to age the same,
And He must win the battle.
                    —MARTIN LUTHER

One day, Lord, You will swallow up death forever.
One day You will bring us home. We praise Your
name!

UNTIL THE DAWN, THIS IS MY PRAYER FOR EACH OF YOU:

Now may the God of peace who brought up our Lord Jesus from the dead, that great Shepherd of the sheep, through the blood of the everlasting covenant, make you complete in every good work to do His will, working in you what is well pleasing in His sight, through Jesus Christ, to whom be glory forever and ever. Amen.
HEBREWS 13:20–21

PART VII

FINDING COMFORT

IN THE SCRIPTURES

Comfort for Those Who Grieve

"Now therefore, do not be afraid;
I will provide for you and your little ones."
And he comforted them and spoke kindly to them.
GENESIS 50:21

Behold, God will not cast away the blameless,
Nor will He uphold the evildoers.
He will yet fill your mouth with laughing,
And your lips with rejoicing.
JOB 8:20–21

But I would strengthen you with my mouth,
And the comfort of my lips
would relieve your grief.
JOB 16:5

The LORD also will be a refuge for the oppressed,
A refuge in times of trouble.
And those who know Your name
will put their trust in You;
For You, LORD,
have not forsaken those who seek You.
PSALM 9:9–10

The Dawn of Hope

The LORD is my rock and
my fortress and my deliverer;
My God, my strength, in whom I will trust;
My shield and the horn of my salvation,
my stronghold.
PSALM 18:2

For He has not despised nor abhorred
the affliction of the afflicted;
Nor has He hidden His face from Him;
But when He cried to Him, He heard.
PSALM 22:24

Oh, love the LORD, all you His saints!
For the LORD preserves the faithful,
And fully repays the proud person.
Be of good courage,
And He shall strengthen your heart,
All you who hope in the LORD.
PSALM 31:23–24

COMFORT FOR THOSE WHO GRIEVE

God is our refuge and strength,
a very present help in trouble.
Therefore we will not fear,
Even though the earth be removed,
And though the mountains be carried
into the midst of the sea;
Though its waters roar
and be troubled,
Though the mountains shake
with its swelling.
PSALM 46:1–3

For this is God,
Our God forever and ever;
He will be our guide
Even to death.
PSALM 48:14

Cast your burden on the LORD,
And He shall sustain you;
He shall never permit
the righteous to be moved.
PSALM 55:22

THE DAWN OF HOPE

Because you have made the LORD,
who is my refuge,
Even the Most High, your dwelling place,
No evil shall befall you,
Nor shall any plague come near your dwelling.
PSALM 91:9–10

"He shall call upon Me, and I will answer him;
I will be with him in trouble;
I will deliver him and honor him.
With long life I will satisfy him,
And show him My salvation."
PSALM 91:15–16

In the multitude of my anxieties within me,
Your comforts delight my soul.
PSALM 94:19

Those who sow in tears
Shall reap in joy.
He who continually goes forth weeping,
Bearing seed for sowing,
Shall doubtless come again with rejoicing,
Bringing his sheaves with him.
PSALM 126:5–6

COMFORT FOR THOSE WHO GRIEVE

Though I walk in the midst of trouble,
You will revive me;
You will stretch out Your hand
Against the wrath of my enemies,
And Your right hand will save me.
PSALM 138:7

How precious also are Your thoughts to me, O God!
How great is the sum of them!
If I should count them,
they would be more in number than the sand;
When I awake, I am still with You.
PSALM 139:17–18

The LORD opens the eyes of the blind;
The LORD raises those who are bowed down;
The LORD loves the righteous.
PSALM 146:8

Sing, O heavens! Be joyful, O earth!
And break out in singing, O mountains!
For the LORD has comforted His people,
And will have mercy on His afflicted.
ISAIAH 49:13

THE DAWN OF HOPE

Have you not known?
Have you not heard?
*The everlasting God, the L*ORD*,*
The Creator of the ends of the earth,
Neither faints nor is weary.
His understanding is unsearchable.
He gives power to the weak,
And to those who have no might
He increases strength.
Even the youths shall faint and be weary,
And the young men shall utterly fall,
*But those who wait on the L*ORD
Shall renew their strength;
They shall mount up with wings like eagles,
They shall run and not be weary,
They shall walk and not faint.
ISAIAH 40:28–31

"I, even I, am He who comforts you.
Who are you that you should be afraid
Of a man who will die,
And of the son of a man who
will be made like grass? . . .
*But I am the L*ORD *your God,*
Who divided the sea whose waves roared—
*The L*ORD *of hosts is His name."*
ISAIAH 51:12, 15

"The Spirit of the Lord GOD is upon Me,
Because the LORD has anointed Me
To preach good tidings to the poor;
He has sent Me to heal the brokenhearted,
To proclaim liberty to the captives,
And the opening of the prison to those who are bound;
To proclaim the acceptable year of the LORD,
And the day of vengeance of our God;
To comfort all who mourn,
To console those who mourn in Zion,
To give them beauty for ashes,
The oil of joy for mourning,
The garment of praise for the spirit of heaviness;
That they may be called trees of righteousness,
The planting of the LORD,
that He may be glorified."
ISAIAH 61:1–3

"As one whom his mother comforts,
So I will comfort you;
And you shall be comforted in Jerusalem."
ISAIAH 66:13

THE DAWN OF HOPE

*And the L*ORD *answered*
the angel who talked to me,
with good and comforting words.
ZECHARIAH 1:13

"Blessed are those who mourn,
For they shall be comforted."
MATTHEW 5:4

"Blessed are those who are
persecuted for righteousness' sake,
For theirs is the kingdom of heaven."
MATTHEW 5:10

"Come to Me, all you who labor and are heavy
laden, and I will give you rest."
MATTHEW 11:28

COMFORT FOR THOSE WHO GRIEVE

*And we know that all things work together
for good to those who love God,
to those who are the called
according to His purpose.*
ROMANS 8:28

*For whatever things were written
before were written for our learning,
that we through the patience and comfort
of the Scriptures might have hope.*
ROMANS 15:4

*Nevertheless God,
who comforts the downcast,
comforted us by the coming of Titus.*
2 CORINTHIANS 7:6

Therefore we have been comforted in your comfort.
2 CORINTHIANS 7:13

Inspirational Library

Beautiful purse/pocket-size editions of Christian classics bound in flexible leatherette. These books make thoughtful gifts for everyone on your list, including yourself!

When I'm on My Knees   The highly popular collection of devotional thoughts on prayer, especially for women.
Flexible Leatherette. $4.97

The Bible Promise Book   Over 1,000 promises from God's Word arranged by topic. What does God promise about matters like: Anger, Illness, Jealousy, Love, Money, Old Age, and Mercy? Find out in this book!
Flexible Leatherette. $3.97

Daily Wisdom for Women   A daily devotional for women seeking biblical wisdom to apply to their lives. Scripture taken from the New American Standard Version of the Bible.
Flexible Leatherette. $4.97

My Daily Prayer Journal   Each page is dated and features a Scripture verse and ample room for you to record your thoughts, prayers, and praises. One page for each day of the year.
Flexible Leatherette. $4.97

Available wherever books are sold.
Or order from:

Barbour Publishing, Inc.
P.O. Box 719
Uhrichsville, OH 44683
http://www.barbourbooks.com

If you order by mail, add $2.00 to your order for shipping.
Prices are subject to change without notice.

MIX-A-MEAL
COOKBOOK

Mixes & Recipes

Deanna Bean & Lorna Shute

Mix-A-Meal Company
Orem, Utah 84097-1662

MIX-A-MEAL Cookbook
c2001 by Mix-A-Meal
c1997 for graphics by Inclipz

Printed in the United States of America

Graphic Design by Roselie Graphics
Original Art Work by WendyJo Originals

If you have any questions or comments concerning this book, please write:
Mix-A-Meal Company
PO Box 971662
Orem, UT 84097-1662

ISBN 0-9708697-0-3 (paperbound)

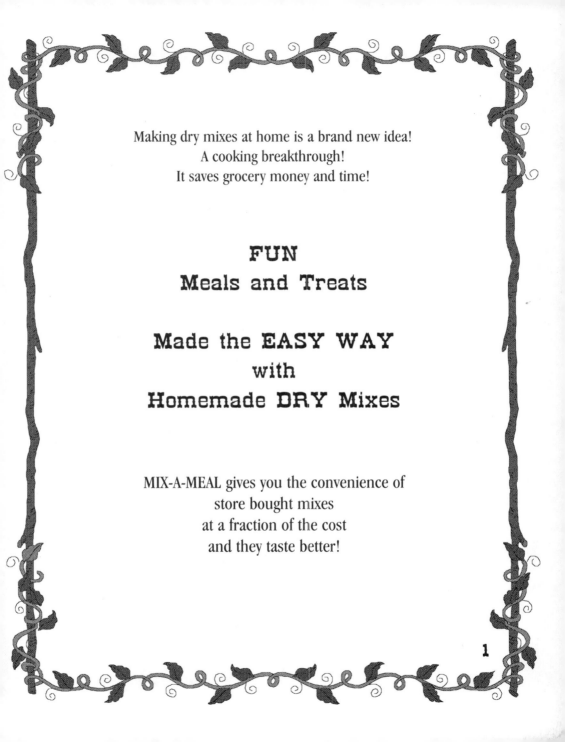

Making dry mixes at home is a brand new idea!
A cooking breakthrough!
It saves grocery money and time!

FUN
Meals and Treats

Made the EASY WAY
with
Homemade DRY Mixes

MIX-A-MEAL gives you the convenience of
store bought mixes
at a fraction of the cost
and they taste better!

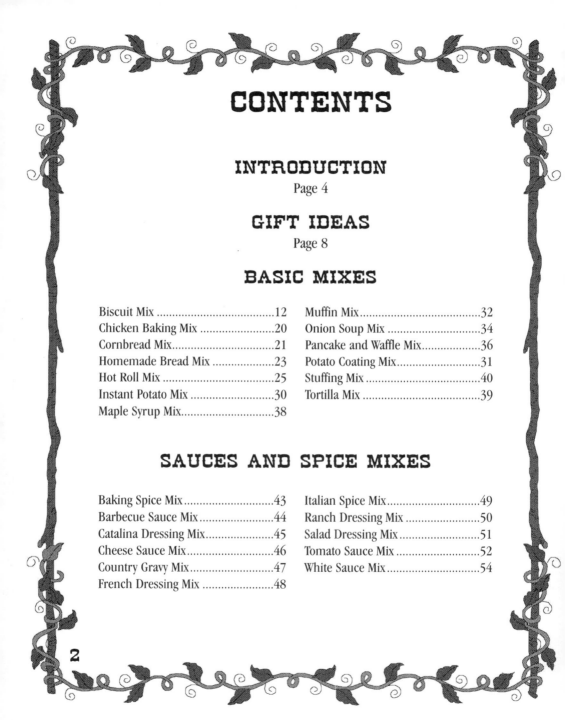

CONTENTS

INTRODUCTION
Page 4

GIFT IDEAS
Page 8

BASIC MIXES

Biscuit Mix 12

Chicken Baking Mix 20

Cornbread Mix................................21

Homemade Bread Mix 23

Hot Roll Mix 25

Instant Potato Mix 30

Maple Syrup Mix.............................38

Muffin Mix.......................................32

Onion Soup Mix 34

Pancake and Waffle Mix..................36

Potato Coating Mix...........................31

Stuffing Mix 40

Tortilla Mix 39

SAUCES AND SPICE MIXES

Baking Spice Mix.............................43

Barbecue Sauce Mix.......................44

Catalina Dressing Mix....................45

Cheese Sauce Mix...........................46

Country Gravy Mix..........................47

French Dressing Mix 48

Italian Spice Mix..............................49

Ranch Dressing Mix 50

Salad Dressing Mix 51

Tomato Sauce Mix 52

White Sauce Mix 54

INSTANT MEALS

Alfredo Delight.................................57
Au gratin Potatoes..........................57
Beef Stroganoff................................59
Broccoli Soup, Cream of 60
Cheddar Hamburger Supper 61
Chili--Thick and Fast 62
Clam Chowder................................60
Coleslaw 63
Lasagna Supreme............................61

Mexican Dinner..............................63
Nacho Potato Bake 62
Oriental Stir Fry.............................64
Potato Soup, Cream of....................60
Quiche 59
Scalloped Potatoes..........................58
Spaghetti Supper 61
Swedish Oven Meatballs 58
Taco Salad 62

EASY FUN DESSERT MIXES

Banana Bread Mix...........................96
Bar Cookie Crust Mix 74
Basic Cookie Mix 66
Brownie Mix 93
Brownies, Whole Wheat Mix...........95
Caramel Lite Mix 82
Chocolate Chip Cookie Mix.............70
Chocolate Pudding Mix...................99
Crumble Topping Mix......................69
Devils Food Cake Mix 89
Frosting, Butter Cream Mix 90

Frosting, Cooked Mix.......................88
Honey Butterscotch Candy Mix 102
Honey Chocolate Candy Mix..........101
Honey Fruit Candy Mix..................103
Ginger Snap Cookie Mix 68
Hot Cocoa Mix 71
Oatmeal Cookie Mix (Honey) 76
Oatmeal Cookie Mix (Sugar) 78
Sugar Cookie Mix............................72
Supermarket Cake Mix 84
Sweetened Condensed Milk Mix 80

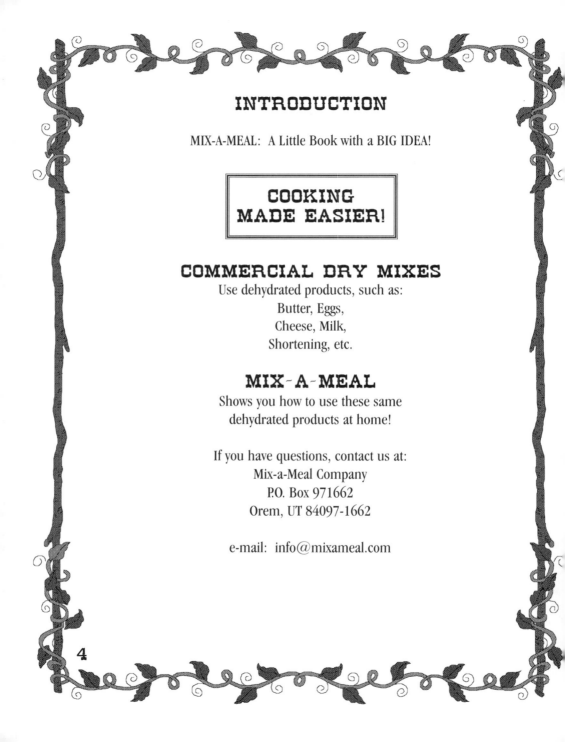

INTRODUCTION

MIX-A-MEAL: A Little Book with a BIG IDEA!

COOKING MADE EASIER!

COMMERCIAL DRY MIXES

Use dehydrated products, such as:
Butter, Eggs,
Cheese, Milk,
Shortening, etc.

MIX-A-MEAL

Shows you how to use these same
dehydrated products at home!

If you have questions, contact us at:
Mix-a-Meal Company
P.O. Box 971662
Orem, UT 84097-1662

e-mail: info@mixameal.com

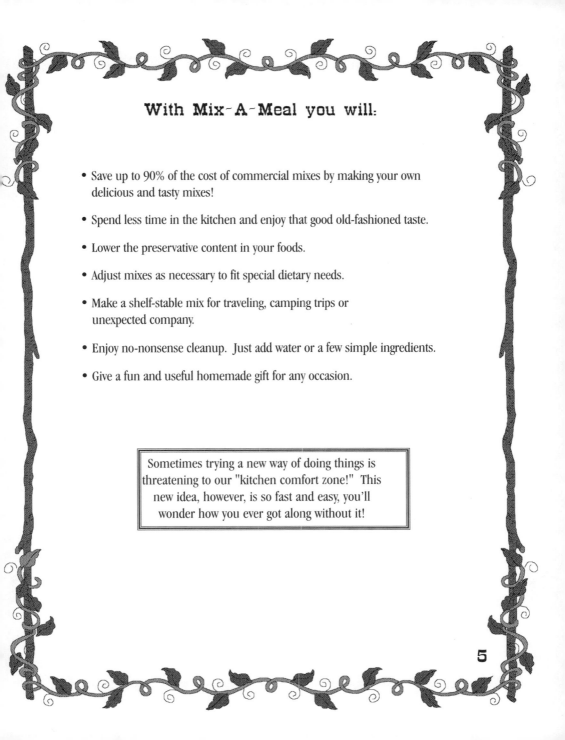

With Mix-A-Meal you will:

- Save up to 90% of the cost of commercial mixes by making your own delicious and tasty mixes!

- Spend less time in the kitchen and enjoy that good old-fashioned taste.

- Lower the preservative content in your foods.

- Adjust mixes as necessary to fit special dietary needs.

- Make a shelf-stable mix for traveling, camping trips or unexpected company.

- Enjoy no-nonsense cleanup. Just add water or a few simple ingredients.

- Give a fun and useful homemade gift for any occasion.

> Sometimes trying a new way of doing things is threatening to our "kitchen comfort zone!" This new idea, however, is so fast and easy, you'll wonder how you ever got along without it!

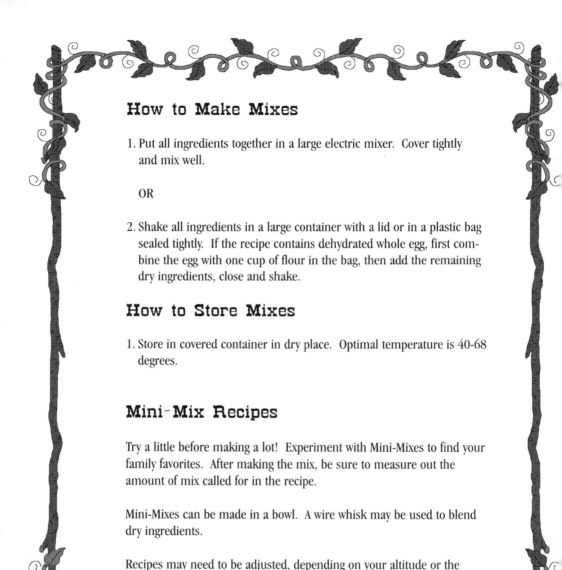

How to Make Mixes

1. Put all ingredients together in a large electric mixer. Cover tightly and mix well.

   OR

2. Shake all ingredients in a large container with a lid or in a plastic bag sealed tightly. If the recipe contains dehydrated whole egg, first combine the egg with one cup of flour in the bag, then add the remaining dry ingredients, close and shake.

How to Store Mixes

1. Store in covered container in dry place. Optimal temperature is 40-68 degrees.

Mini-Mix Recipes

Try a little before making a lot! Experiment with Mini-Mixes to find your family favorites. After making the mix, be sure to measure out the amount of mix called for in the recipe.

Mini-Mixes can be made in a bowl. A wire whisk may be used to blend dry ingredients.

Recipes may need to be adjusted, depending on your altitude or the brand of dehydrated food you use (another reason to try the Mini-Mix before making the full mix).

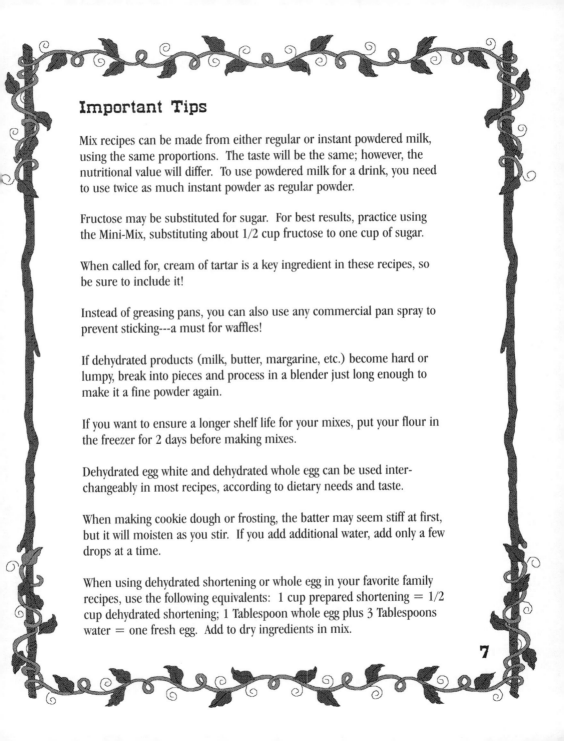

Important Tips

Mix recipes can be made from either regular or instant powdered milk, using the same proportions. The taste will be the same; however, the nutritional value will differ. To use powdered milk for a drink, you need to use twice as much instant powder as regular powder.

Fructose may be substituted for sugar. For best results, practice using the Mini-Mix, substituting about 1/2 cup fructose to one cup of sugar.

When called for, cream of tartar is a key ingredient in these recipes, so be sure to include it!

Instead of greasing pans, you can also use any commercial pan spray to prevent sticking---a must for waffles!

If dehydrated products (milk, butter, margarine, etc.) become hard or lumpy, break into pieces and process in a blender just long enough to make it a fine powder again.

If you want to ensure a longer shelf life for your mixes, put your flour in the freezer for 2 days before making mixes.

Dehydrated egg white and dehydrated whole egg can be used inter-changeably in most recipes, according to dietary needs and taste.

When making cookie dough or frosting, the batter may seem stiff at first, but it will moisten as you stir. If you add additional water, add only a few drops at a time.

When using dehydrated shortening or whole egg in your favorite family recipes, use the following equivalents: 1 cup prepared shortening = 1/2 cup dehydrated shortening; 1 Tablespoon whole egg plus 3 Tablespoons water = one fresh egg. Add to dry ingredients in mix.

GIFT IDEAS

Looking for a terrific, useful gift? Make a Mix-a-Meal gift for any occasion. The possibilities are endless for Bridal Showers, Weddings, Valentine's Day, Birthdays, Anniversaries, Christmas, and more.

Here are some fun ideas:

Place a Mix-A-Meal Cookbook and ingredients for a recipe in a gift basket, along with utensils, serving spoons, etc.

Put a cookie mix in a decorated cloth bag or decorated box with cookie cutters dangling from ribbon.

Layer ingredients of cookie, cake, or brownie mixes in clear jars. Do not mix together. Top with fabric-decorated lid and add ribbon or raffia. Include directions for using mix.

Here is a fun gift for kids:

PLAY DOUGH MIX
Combine:
6 cups flour
3 cups salt
2 Tbsp. cream of tartar

MINI-MIX
Combine:
1 1/2 cups flour
3/4 cups salt
1 1/2 tsp. cream of tartar

Add desired food coloring to 1 1/2 cups water and 1 1/2 Tbsp. oil. Add 2 1/4 cups Play Dough Mix (above). Bring to a boil, stirring, until mixture forms a thick ball. Knead to desired texture. Store in covered container.

CAMPING IDEAS

Summer camping trips are a snap when you plan ahead with Mix-A-Meal. Make the mixes before the trip and put them in ziplock bags with the directions written on the bag. Here are some fun meal ideas:

Breakfast:
Pancakes (p. 36) with Maple Syrup (p. 38)
Biscuits (p. 13) in Dutch Oven with Country Gravy (p. 47)

Lunch:
Cream of Broccoli Soup (p. 60)
Alfredo Delight (p. 57)
Pocket Bread (p. 28) (make ahead and freeze) with fillings (p. 29)

Dinner:
Barbecue Sauce (p. 44) for any barbecued meat or veggies
Spaghetti Supper (p. 61)

Desserts:
Chocolate Pudding (p. 100) - Refrigerate in ice chest or in cold stream (put rocks around it so the pudding won't float away!)

Yellow Cake (p. 85) in Dutch Oven with melted butter, brown sugar, and pineapple in bottom for Pineapple Upside Down Cake

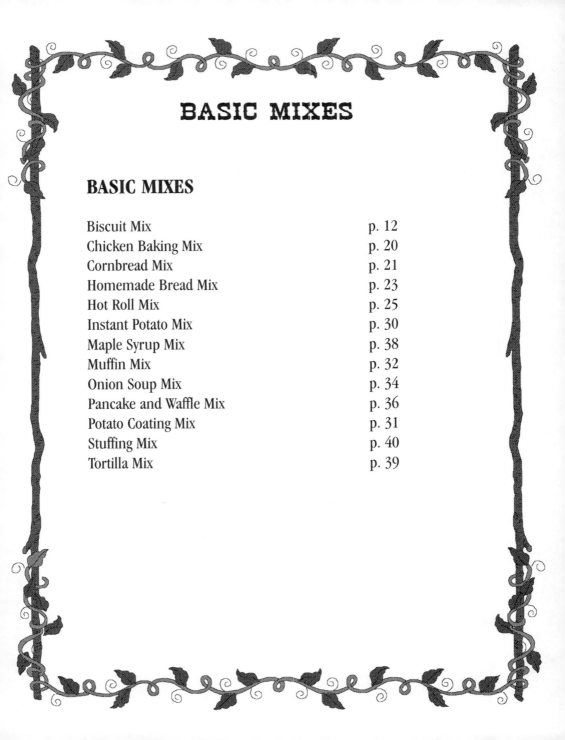

BASIC MIXES

BASIC MIXES

Biscuit Mix	p. 12
Chicken Baking Mix	p. 20
Cornbread Mix	p. 21
Homemade Bread Mix	p. 23
Hot Roll Mix	p. 25
Instant Potato Mix	p. 30
Maple Syrup Mix	p. 38
Muffin Mix	p. 32
Onion Soup Mix	p. 34
Pancake and Waffle Mix	p. 36
Potato Coating Mix	p. 31
Stuffing Mix	p. 40
Tortilla Mix	p. 39

BISCUIT MIX

Combine:

8 1/2 cups flour
1 1/4 cups dehydrated shortening or margarine
3/4 cup powdered milk
1/2 cup dehydrated whole egg
1/4 cup baking powder
1 Tbsp. salt
2 tsp. cream of tartar
1 tsp. baking soda

MINI-MIX

Combine:

2 1/8 cups flour
5 Tbsp. dehydrated shortening or margarine
3 Tbsp. powdered milk
2 Tbsp. dehydrated whole egg
1 scant Tbsp. baking powder
1 tsp. salt
1/2 tsp. cream of tartar
1/4 tsp. baking soda

Drop Biscuits

Combine:

3 cups Biscuit Mix (above)
1 cup water

Stir vigorously until blended and drop by teaspoonsful onto greased baking sheet. Bake at 400 degrees for 10-12 minutes. Makes 12-18 biscuits.

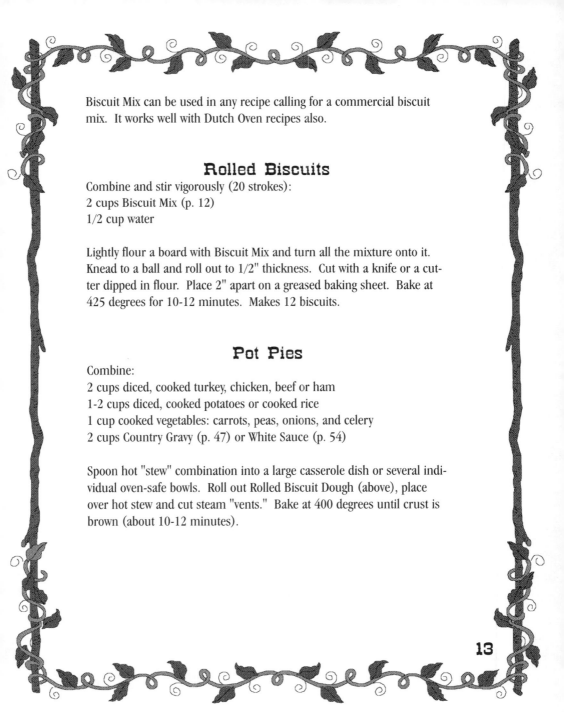

Biscuit Mix can be used in any recipe calling for a commercial biscuit mix. It works well with Dutch Oven recipes also.

Rolled Biscuits

Combine and stir vigorously (20 strokes):
2 cups Biscuit Mix (p. 12)
1/2 cup water

Lightly flour a board with Biscuit Mix and turn all the mixture onto it. Knead to a ball and roll out to 1/2" thickness. Cut with a knife or a cutter dipped in flour. Place 2" apart on a greased baking sheet. Bake at 425 degrees for 10-12 minutes. Makes 12 biscuits.

Pot Pies

Combine:
2 cups diced, cooked turkey, chicken, beef or ham
1-2 cups diced, cooked potatoes or cooked rice
1 cup cooked vegetables: carrots, peas, onions, and celery
2 cups Country Gravy (p. 47) or White Sauce (p. 54)

Spoon hot "stew" combination into a large casserole dish or several individual oven-safe bowls. Roll out Rolled Biscuit Dough (above), place over hot stew and cut steam "vents." Bake at 400 degrees until crust is brown (about 10-12 minutes).

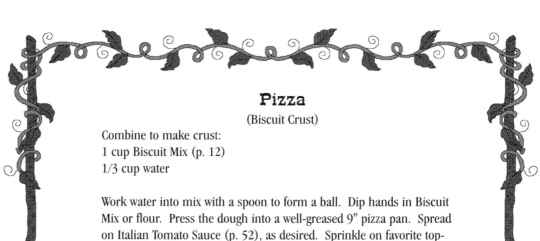

Pizza
(Biscuit Crust)

Combine to make crust:
1 cup Biscuit Mix (p. 12)
1/3 cup water

Work water into mix with a spoon to form a ball. Dip hands in Biscuit Mix or flour. Press the dough into a well-greased 9" pizza pan. Spread on Italian Tomato Sauce (p. 52), as desired. Sprinkle on favorite toppings, finish with grated cheese. Bake at 400 degrees for 10-12 minutes. Makes one 9" pizza.

Mexican Pizza

Make Pizza Crust (above) and make Mexican Sauce (p. 63). Cover crust with sauce and top with a layer of refried beans. Add crumble-fried hamburger and finish with a layer of grated cheese. Bake at 425 degrees for 10-12 minutes. Top with shredded lettuce, thinly-sliced onions and tomatoes. Garnish with sour cream.

Fruit Breakfast Pizza

Combine:
2 cups Biscuit Mix (p. 12)
1/3 cup sugar
1/2 cup, plus 3 Tbsp. water

Make Pizza Crust (above) and spread onto large pizza pan or cookie sheet. Arrange 4 cups cooked, drained apples or peaches on top of crust. Top with 1-2 cups Crumble Topping Mix (p. 69). Bake at 400 degrees for 15 minutes. Serve with whipped cream.

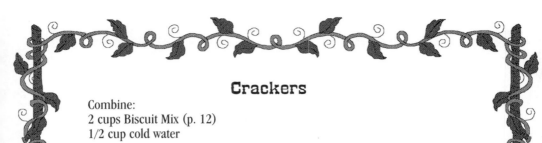

Crackers

Combine:
2 cups Biscuit Mix (p. 12)
1/2 cup cold water

Mix as for Rolled Biscuits, only roll out VERY THIN. Shake a little salt over the rolled dough. Cut with pizza cutter into 4 pieces. Lift with spatula onto greased baking sheet. Cut again with pizza cutter into small pieces about 1/2" square. Bake at 425 degrees for 7-10 minutes.

Caution: Do not over bake crackers; they will crisp as they cool.

VARIATIONS:

CHEESY SNACKS:
2 cups Biscuit Mix (p. 12)
1/4 cup dehydrated cheese
1/2 cup, plus 2 tsp. water

ONION CRACKERS:
2 cups Biscuit Mix (p. 12)
2 tsp. Onion Soup Mix (p. 34)
1/2 cup, plus 2 tsp. water

TACO CRISPS:
2 cups Biscuit Mix (p. 12)
1/2 tsp. taco spices and 1/2 cup water
Shake on seasoned salt (p. 43) before baking

VEGETABLE THINS:
2 cups Biscuit Mix (p. 12)
2 tsp. veggie salt mix (p. 49)
1/2 cup, plus 1 tsp. water

WHOLE WHEAT:
Use Biscuit Mix (p. 12) made with all or part whole wheat flour.
Sprinkle with salt before baking.

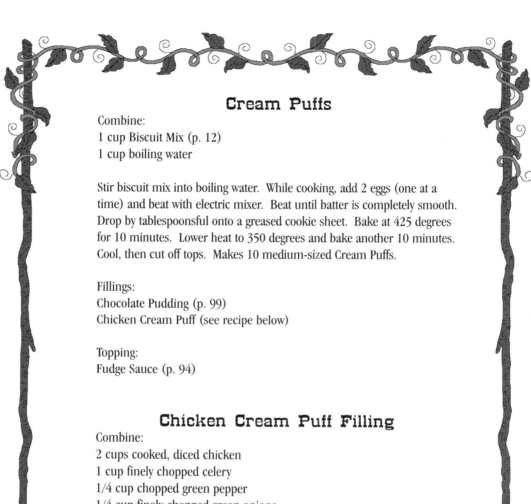

Cream Puffs

Combine:
1 cup Biscuit Mix (p. 12)
1 cup boiling water

Stir biscuit mix into boiling water. While cooking, add 2 eggs (one at a time) and beat with electric mixer. Beat until batter is completely smooth. Drop by tablespoonsful onto a greased cookie sheet. Bake at 425 degrees for 10 minutes. Lower heat to 350 degrees and bake another 10 minutes. Cool, then cut off tops. Makes 10 medium-sized Cream Puffs.

Fillings:
Chocolate Pudding (p. 99)
Chicken Cream Puff (see recipe below)

Topping:
Fudge Sauce (p. 94)

Chicken Cream Puff Filling

Combine:
2 cups cooked, diced chicken
1 cup finely chopped celery
1/4 cup chopped green pepper
1/4 cup finely chopped green onions
1 can sliced water chestnuts (optional)
1 Tbsp. lemon juice
Mayonnaise to desired consistency
Top with sprouts, if desired

Tempura

(this batter makes wonderful, fast onion rings!)

Combine:
3 cups Biscuit Mix (p. 12)
2 scant cups cold water

Slice vegetables thin or meats to bite size and dip into batter:

Zucchini	Onion Slices	Carrots
Parsnips	Green Peppers	Apples
Yams	Mushrooms	Eggplant
Shrimp	Fish	Cheese Cubes

Fry in hot oil, turning once to brown both sides.

Fritters

Combine:
1 cup Biscuit Mix (p. 12)
1/2 cup diced apples, onions, clams or corn
1/4 cup liquid

Drop by teaspoonful into hot oil and fry golden brown on each side.

Braided Dinner Roll

Combine and stir vigorously 20 strokes:
2 cups Biscuit Mix (p. 12)
1/2 cup cold water

Turn mixture onto a board floured with additional Biscuit Mix. Knead lightly and roll dough into an 11" x 14" rectangle pan. Place on lightly-greased cookie sheet. Choose a filling (p. 18) and spoon it down the center of the dough. Cut diagonal strips at 1" intervals from the outside edge to the filling. Fold strips to cross over the top of the filling. Bake at 375 degrees for 15-20 minutes and top with a sauce.

Braided Roll Fillings

Chicken OR Tuna Filling

Combine:
1 can chunk tuna, drained or 1 cup cooked, diced chicken
1/2 cup chopped ripe olives
1/2 cup chopped celery
1/2 cup chopped green pepper
1/2 cup chopped green onions
1/2 cup grated cheese
1/4 cup cream of chicken soup or 1/3 cup White Sauce (p. 54)
After baking, serve with a sauce:
Cheese Sauce (p. 46)
White Sauce (p. 54) or remaining cream of chicken soup

Patty-Melt Filling

Combine:
crumble-fried hamburger
sliced olives
green peppers
sliced onions
swiss cheese
Add:
Tomato sauce (p. 52), Picante' sauce (p. 53), Chili Thick and Fast (p. 62)
After baking, serve with additional sauce.

Pork & Beans Picnic

Drain pork and beans and save sauce for topping.
Add hot dog slices and cheese to beans for filling.

Taco Filling

Combine:
refried beans
crumble-fried hamburger
grated cheese
Picante' sauce (p. 53)
Top with tossed salad and sour cream over each slice.

Breakfast Cake

Combine and mix well:
3 cups Biscuit Mix (p. 12)
1/3 cup sugar
1 1/4 cups water
2 tsp. liquid vanilla

Spread half of the batter into a greased and floured 9" x 9" pan. Add slices of drained, cooked or canned apples or peaches.

Sprinkle 3/4 cup Crumble Topping Mix (p. 69) over the fruit. Add remaining batter and top with 1/4 cup Crumble Topping Mix. Bake at 350 degrees for 40 minutes. Serve hot with whipped cream.

Note: THIS CAKE CAN ALSO BE PREPARED AND REFRIGERATED OVERNIGHT:

Make the cake as directed above. Cover with plastic wrap and place in the refrigerator. The next morning, bake, uncovered, as directed above.

A FUN SPECIAL BREAKFAST WITH NO MORNING FUSS!

CHICKEN BAKING MIX

Combine:

3 cups flour
2 Tbsp. dehydrated margarine or butter
2 Tbsp. chicken bouillon (soup base)
1 Tbsp. poultry seasoning
1 Tbsp. dehydrated cheese
1 tsp. onion powder
1/4 tsp. garlic powder
1/4 tsp. black pepper

MINI-MIX

Contents:

1 scant cup flour
2 tsp. dehydrated margarine or butter
2 tsp. chicken bouillon (soup base)
1 tsp. dehydrated cheese
1 tsp. poultry seasoning
1/4 tsp. onion powder
pinch of garlic powder
pinch of black pepper

Oven Baked Chicken

Combine:

6-8 pieces chicken
1 cup Chicken Baking Mix in a plastic bag

Dip chicken in water, milk, or whipped egg (for a thicker coating). Shake chicken pieces in a plastic bag, one at a time, to coat with mix. Bake at 350 degrees on foil-lined cookie sheet for 1 hour or until golden brown.

CORNBREAD MIX

Combine:

5 cups whole wheat or white flour
5 cups cornmeal
3 1/3 cups white or brown sugar
1 1/3 cups dehydrated margarine or butter
1/4 cup powdered milk or powdered buttermilk
1/2 cup dehydrated egg white or whole egg*
2 1/2 tsp. baking soda
2 1/2 tsp. baking powder
2 1/2 tsp. salt

MINI-MIX

Combine:

1 1/4 cup whole wheat or white flour
1 1/4 cup cornmeal
3/4 cup white or brown sugar
1/3 rounded cup dehydrated margarine or shortening
2 Tbsp. powdered milk or powdered buttermilk
1 1/2 Tbsp. dehydrated egg white or whole egg*
1/2 rounded tsp. baking soda
1/2 rounded tsp. baking powder
1/2 tsp. salt

*Using dehydrated egg white instead of dehydrated whole egg gives the cornbread a lighter taste, but either works well. You can also leave the dehydrated egg out of the mix and whip 1 fresh egg as part of the liquid measurement.

NOTE: You can grind whole dried corn in your wheat grinder to make your own finely-textured cornmeal. It is recommended that you grind at least 1 cup of wheat afterwards to clean the grinder stones.

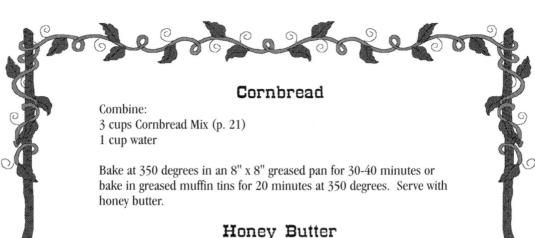

Cornbread

Combine:
3 cups Cornbread Mix (p. 21)
1 cup water

Bake at 350 degrees in an 8" x 8" greased pan for 30-40 minutes or bake in greased muffin tins for 20 minutes at 350 degrees. Serve with honey butter.

Honey Butter

Stir together:
1 cup honey
1/2 cup dehydrated butter

High-Rise Cornbread

Combine:
3 cups Cornbread Mix (p. 21)
2 cups fresh buttermilk

Bake in an 8" x 8" greased pan at 350 degrees for 30-40 minutes.

Cornbread Plus

Combine:
2 Tbsp. dehydrated egg white
1/4 cup water

Whip for 1 minute until peaks form. Lumps will dissolve as egg whites are whipped.

Add:
3 cups Cornbread Mix (p. 21)
1 cup water

Fold into whipped egg whites. Bake in an 8" x 8" greased pan at 350 degrees for 30-40 minutes.

HOMEMADE BREAD MIX

Combine:
8 cups sugar
4 cups dehydrated shortening
1 cup salt

Note: This mix makes over 60 loaves of either white or whole wheat bread!

MINI-MIX

Combine:
1/2 cup sugar
1/4 cup dehydrated shortening
1 Tbsp. salt

Homemade Bread

Sprinkle 2 Tablespoons yeast into 2 cups warm water. Let stand until yeast dissolves and begins to foam.

Add:
3 cups warm water
3/4 cups Homemade Bread Mix (above)
3/4 cups vital wheat gluten, optional

Knead in about 10-11 cups of flour to make a soft dough. Continue kneading for 8-10 minutes. Shape and place in four well-greased medium-sized bread pans. Let rise until double in bulk, about 25-45 minutes. Bake at 350 degrees for 30-35 minutes. Remove loaves from pans and place side by side on a towel. Cover completely with the towel and place on a rack to cool. Makes 4 medium loaves.

Scones: Pinch off desired amount of dough and roll to 1/4" thickness. Cut into desired shapes and fry in hot grease until browned.

Note: Store yeast in the freezer for longer life.

Bread Maker Whole Wheat Bread

If you have a single loaf Bread Maker, you will love this mix!

Combine ingredients in your bread maker pan in this order:
1 1/4 cups water
1/4 cup Homemade Bread Mix (p. 23)
3 cups white bread flour
2 tsp. active dry yeast

Bake according to bread maker's instructions.

For whole wheat bread, follow above instructions combining:
2 1/2 cups whole wheat flour (Golden 86 wheat flour works great!)
1/2 cup vital wheat gluten
2 tsp. active dry yeast

Why Use Gluten?

Gluten is the ingredient that gives bread a finer texture and allows it to rise higher, especially in a bread maker. It is one of the key ingredients in costly individual bread mixes.

HOT ROLL MIX

Combine:
10 cups flour
1 cup dehydrated margarine or butter
2/3 cups sugar
1/4 cup powdered milk
2 Tbsp. salt

MINI-MIX

Combine:
3 1/3 cups flour
1/3 cup dehydrated margarine or butter
1/4 cup sugar
1 heaping Tbsp. powdered milk
2 tsp. salt

Note: A 30-pound plastic storage bucket holds four Hot Roll Mixes. Just prepare a regular mix and pour it into the bucket. Repeat this process three more times and the bucket will be full, a MAXI-MIX!

Basic Roll Dough

Combine:
1 1/2 cups warm water
1 Tbsp. active dry yeast

Add a sprinkle of sugar to activate yeast (optional). Let rise for 3-5 minutes.

Add:
4 cups Hot Roll Mix (above)

Knead 5-10 minutes until smooth and satiny. Let rise in a bowl for one hour (this step is optional). Roll out and shape rolls on a greased baking sheet
OR
Pinch off in 3" rounds and place side-by-side in a greased 9" x 13" pan. Let rise for one hour or until double in size. Bake at 375 degrees for 15 minutes. Lightly cover with foil the last 5 minutes.

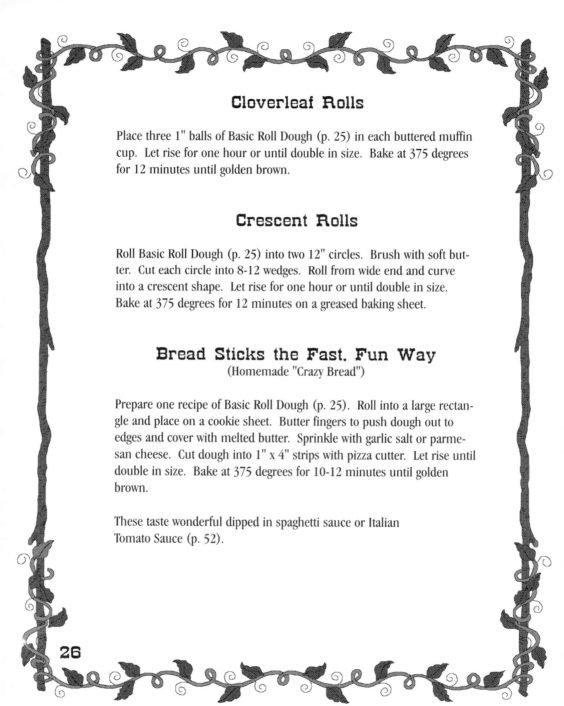

Cloverleaf Rolls

Place three 1" balls of Basic Roll Dough (p. 25) in each buttered muffin cup. Let rise for one hour or until double in size. Bake at 375 degrees for 12 minutes until golden brown.

Crescent Rolls

Roll Basic Roll Dough (p. 25) into two 12" circles. Brush with soft butter. Cut each circle into 8-12 wedges. Roll from wide end and curve into a crescent shape. Let rise for one hour or until double in size. Bake at 375 degrees for 12 minutes on a greased baking sheet.

Bread Sticks the Fast, Fun Way
(Homemade "Crazy Bread")

Prepare one recipe of Basic Roll Dough (p. 25). Roll into a large rectangle and place on a cookie sheet. Butter fingers to push dough out to edges and cover with melted butter. Sprinkle with garlic salt or parmesan cheese. Cut dough into 1" x 4" strips with pizza cutter. Let rise until double in size. Bake at 375 degrees for 10-12 minutes until golden brown.

These taste wonderful dipped in spaghetti sauce or Italian Tomato Sauce (p. 52).

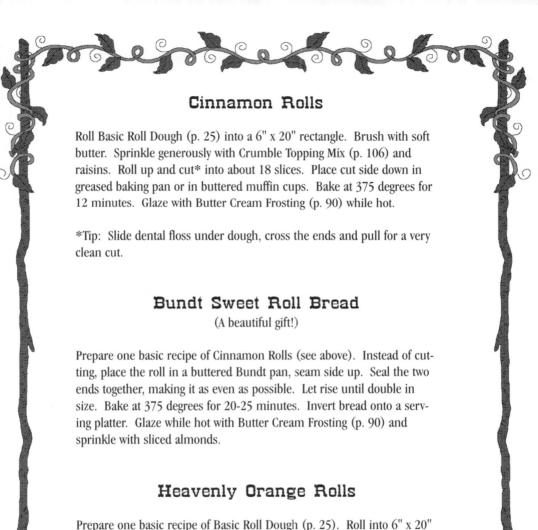

Cinnamon Rolls

Roll Basic Roll Dough (p. 25) into a 6" x 20" rectangle. Brush with soft butter. Sprinkle generously with Crumble Topping Mix (p. 106) and raisins. Roll up and cut* into about 18 slices. Place cut side down in greased baking pan or in buttered muffin cups. Bake at 375 degrees for 12 minutes. Glaze with Butter Cream Frosting (p. 90) while hot.

*Tip: Slide dental floss under dough, cross the ends and pull for a very clean cut.

Bundt Sweet Roll Bread
(A beautiful gift!)

Prepare one basic recipe of Cinnamon Rolls (see above). Instead of cutting, place the roll in a buttered Bundt pan, seam side up. Seal the two ends together, making it as even as possible. Let rise until double in size. Bake at 375 degrees for 20-25 minutes. Invert bread onto a serving platter. Glaze while hot with Butter Cream Frosting (p. 90) and sprinkle with sliced almonds.

Heavenly Orange Rolls

Prepare one basic recipe of Basic Roll Dough (p. 25). Roll into 6" x 20" rectangle and spread with melted butter. Sprinkle with 1/3 to 1/2 cup sugar. Add grated peel from 1 large orange or 1/3 cup orange granules.

Place in muffin tins with one teaspoon of melted butter in each muffin cup. Let rise until double in size. Bake at 375 degrees for 10-12 minutes. Glaze while hot with Lemon Butter Cream Glaze (p. 91).

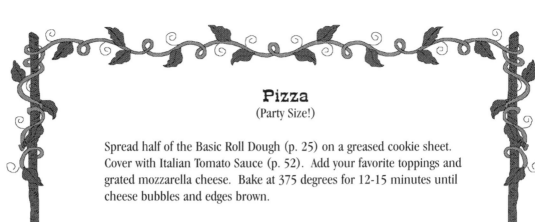

Pizza
(Party Size!)

Spread half of the Basic Roll Dough (p. 25) on a greased cookie sheet. Cover with Italian Tomato Sauce (p. 52). Add your favorite toppings and grated mozzarella cheese. Bake at 375 degrees for 12-15 minutes until cheese bubbles and edges brown.

Tips: Grease pan or sprinkle cornmeal on the pan for easy crust removal. Grease your hands to press the dough out evenly in the pan.

Pocket Bread

Combine:
3/4 cup warm water
1/2 Tbsp. yeast

Yeast will activate faster with a little sugar sprinkled on top. Combine and let stand for 3-5 minutes. Add 2 cups Hot Roll Mix (p. 25). Knead 5-10 minutes. Cover and let rise for one hour. Divide dough into six 3" balls and place on a greased baking sheet. Roll with the side of a glass or press out with fingers to 4" circles. Bake immediately in 400-degree oven for 5 to 7 minutes. Let cool 10 minutes before cutting tops (kitchen scissors work great!). Stuff with your choice of Pocket Bread Fillings (p. 29).

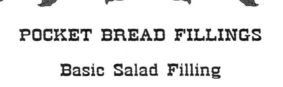

POCKET BREAD FILLINGS

Basic Salad Filling

Combine any of the following (finely sliced):
Lettuce, cucumbers, avocado, tomatoes, celery, green onions, green peppers, mushrooms, alfalfa sprouts.

Mix vegetables together with mayonnaise and lemon juice
OR
Layer vegetables in the pocket bread and top with favorite dressing.
Garnish with grated cheese.

Deluxe Pocket Bread Fillings

Add to Basic Salad Filling (above) cooked, diced chicken, ham, bacon, chipped beef or hard-boiled eggs. Garnish with chicken or bacon textured vegetable protein (TVP), optional.

Taco Filling

Layer in the pocket bread:
crumble-fried hamburger
grated cheese
shredded lettuce
Picanté Sauce (p. 53)
Bean Dip (p. 53)

Top with sour cream.

INSTANT POTATO MIX
Combine:
6 scant cups dehydrated margarine
3 cups powdered milk
1/2 scant cup salt
1/3 cup dehydrated cheese
1 Tbsp. onion powder

MINI-MIX
Combine:
3 Tbsp. dehydrated margarine
1 1/2 Tbsp. powdered milk
3/4 tsp. salt
1/2 tsp. dehydrated cheese
1/8 tsp. onion powder

Instant Potatoes
(Use this mix instead of adding fresh milk and butter to instant potatoes)

Combine with wire whisk:
1 1/2 cups hottest tap water (adjust water, if needed, for the brand of potatoes used)
1/4 cup Instant Potato Mix (above)

Add:
1 cup instant potato flakes. Cover and let sit for a minute. Stir gently and serve.

Option: For a wonderful flavor, fold in 2 Tbsp. Dip for Chips or Veggies (p. 34).

Fresh Mashed Potatoes

When whipping fresh cooked potatoes, add Instant Potato Mix (above) and water to desired flavor and consistency. Potatoes will have a creamy, rich texture.

POTATO COATING MIX

Combine:

2 cups dehydrated cheese

1/2 cup dehydrated butter or margarine

3 Tbsp. beef bouillon (soup base)

3 Tbsp. onion powder

3 Tbsp. dried parsley

1 1/2 Tbsp. paprika

1 tsp. garlic powder

1 tsp. pepper

MINI-MIX

Combine:

2 Tbsp. dehydrated cheese

1/2 Tbsp. dehydrated butter or margarine

1 tsp. beef bouillon (soup base)

1 tsp. onion powder

1 tsp. dried parsley

1/2 tsp. paprika

1/8 tsp. garlic powder

1/8 tsp. pepper

Oven-Fried Potatoes

Peel and dice 6 medium potatoes. Pour 2 Tbsp. cooking oil (or water) into a plastic bag. Add potatoes and coat pieces. Process 2 slices of toast in a blender to make fine bread crumbs. Add bread crumbs and 1/4 cup Potato Coating Mix (above) to bag and shake. Place potatoes on a sprayed cookie sheet. Bake at 375 degrees for 30 minutes.

Variation: Add 1 Tbsp. taco seasoning.

MUFFIN MIX

Combine:

8 cups white or whole wheat flour
2 1/2 cups brown or white sugar
1 1/4 cups dehydrated shortening
1/2 cup powdered milk
1/3 cup baking powder
1 1/2 tsp. salt

MINI-MIX

Combine:

2 1/4 cups white or whole wheat flour
1/3 cup brown or white sugar
1/4 cup dehydrated shortening
3 Tbsp. powdered milk
1 1/2 Tbsp. baking powder
1/2 scant tsp. salt

Muffins

Blend one fresh egg and enough water to make 2 cups liquid. Add 3 1/8
cups Muffin Mix (above). Blend well with a wire whisk, but do not beat.
Fill 9-10 buttered muffin cups almost full. Bake 20 minutes at 425 degrees.
OR
Spread in an 8" x 8" greased pan. Bake at 400 degrees for 25-35 minutes.

Optional: Before baking, add 1/2 cup raisins or blueberries or top with
brown sugar and chopped nuts.

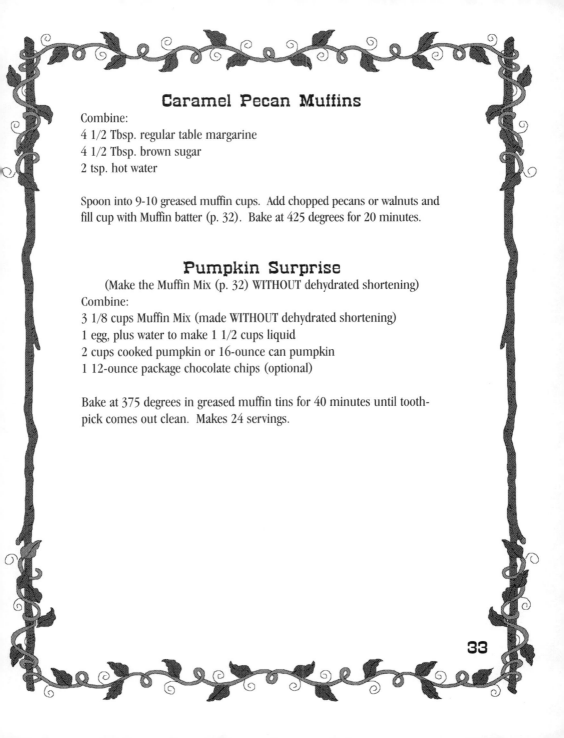

Caramel Pecan Muffins

Combine:

4 1/2 Tbsp. regular table margarine
4 1/2 Tbsp. brown sugar
2 tsp. hot water

Spoon into 9-10 greased muffin cups. Add chopped pecans or walnuts and fill cup with Muffin batter (p. 32). Bake at 425 degrees for 20 minutes.

Pumpkin Surprise

(Make the Muffin Mix (p. 32) WITHOUT dehydrated shortening)

Combine:

3 1/8 cups Muffin Mix (made WITHOUT dehydrated shortening)
1 egg, plus water to make 1 1/2 cups liquid
2 cups cooked pumpkin or 16-ounce can pumpkin
1 12-ounce package chocolate chips (optional)

Bake at 375 degrees in greased muffin tins for 40 minutes until toothpick comes out clean. Makes 24 servings.

ONION SOUP MIX

Combine:

2/3 cup dehydrated chopped onions
1/2 cup beef bouillon (soup base)
1/2 cup dehydrated butter or margarine
2 Tbsp. cornstarch
2 tsp. onion powder
2 tsp. parsley flakes (optional)

Mix well and store in quart jar. Use in any dry onion soup recipe.

Dip for Chips or Veggies

Combine:

2 tsp. Onion Soup Mix (above)
1 cup (8 oz.) sour cream (fat free works great!)

Onion Steamed Rice

Combine:

1 cup rice to 3 cups water
2 tsp. Onion Soup Mix (above)

Cover and steam 20 minutes until rice is tender and dry.

Pasta Perfect

Combine:

1 Tbsp. butter
2 tsp. Onion Soup Mix (above)

Saute' one minute and add 2 cups cooked fettuccine or egg noodles. Stir until warmed through and serve.

Roast Beef Supreme

Sprinkle 1-2 tsp. Onion Soup Mix (p. 34) into crock pot. Place a 3-4 pound beef roast on top of the mix. Sprinkle 1-2 tsp. Onion Soup Mix over the top of the roast. Add 2 cups water and cover. Cook for 8-12 hours on medium heat.
OR
Cook for 3 hours on high, and then 6-8 more hours on low.

French Onion Soup

Combine:
1 cup water
1/2 cup Caramelized Onions (see recipe below)
2 tsp. Onion Soup Mix (p. 34)

Caramelized Onions

Cook fresh, chopped onions or thinly-sliced onions with a little water in a pan and let them boil dry. Watch carefully, and as soon as they begin to brown, add a little more water. As you stir the onions in the water, they will absorb the brown from the bottom of the pan, giving them a sweet, beefy flavor. You can repeat this procedure as many times as you wish for desired tenderness. These onions add a wonderful flavor to any homemade soup or stew.

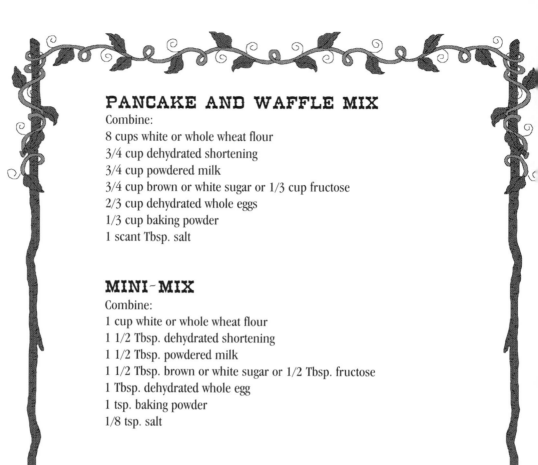

PANCAKE AND WAFFLE MIX

Combine:
8 cups white or whole wheat flour
3/4 cup dehydrated shortening
3/4 cup powdered milk
3/4 cup brown or white sugar or 1/3 cup fructose
2/3 cup dehydrated whole eggs
1/3 cup baking powder
1 scant Tbsp. salt

MINI-MIX

Combine:
1 cup white or whole wheat flour
1 1/2 Tbsp. dehydrated shortening
1 1/2 Tbsp. powdered milk
1 1/2 Tbsp. brown or white sugar or 1/2 Tbsp. fructose
1 Tbsp. dehydrated whole egg
1 tsp. baking powder
1/8 tsp. salt

Pancakes or Waffles
(Light & Fluffy!)

Combine:
1 scant cup Pancake Mix (above)
1 cup water

Let stand a minute and cook on a hot, oiled griddle. Try spooning pancakes with a gravy ladle for uniform size. Turn when bubbles break on top. Makes six 4" pancakes. Serve with homemade Maple Syrup (p. 38).

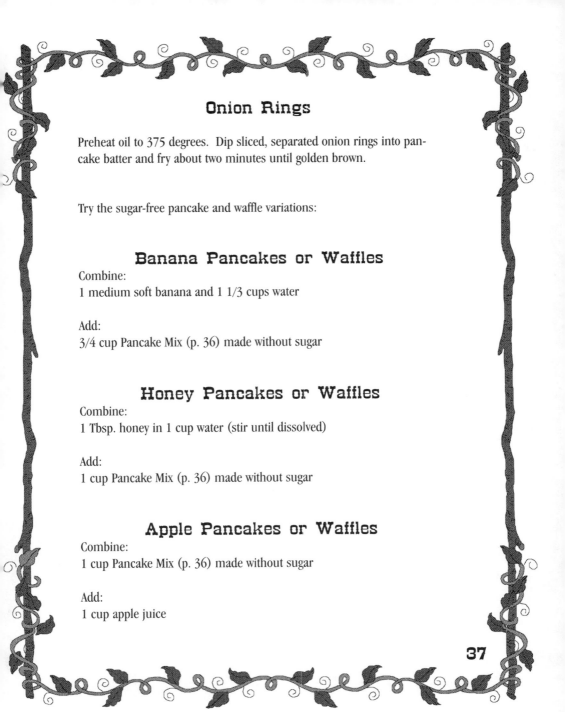

Onion Rings

Preheat oil to 375 degrees. Dip sliced, separated onion rings into pancake batter and fry about two minutes until golden brown.

Try the sugar-free pancake and waffle variations:

Banana Pancakes or Waffles

Combine:
1 medium soft banana and 1 1/3 cups water

Add:
3/4 cup Pancake Mix (p. 36) made without sugar

Honey Pancakes or Waffles

Combine:
1 Tbsp. honey in 1 cup water (stir until dissolved)

Add:
1 cup Pancake Mix (p. 36) made without sugar

Apple Pancakes or Waffles

Combine:
1 cup Pancake Mix (p. 36) made without sugar

Add:
1 cup apple juice

37

MAPLE SYRUP MIX
Combine:
6 cups white sugar
2 cups brown sugar
1 tsp. powdered maple syrup flavoring
1/2 tsp. powdered vanilla flavoring

MINI-MIX
Combine:
1 1/2 cups white sugar
1/2 cup brown sugar
1/4 tsp. powdered maple syrup flavoring
1/8 tsp. powdered vanilla flavoring

Maple Syrup
Combine:
2 cups Maple Syrup Mix
1 cup water

Stir until mixture boils. Cover and simmer gently for 10 minutes. Syrup will thicken when refrigerated.

Maple Syrup
(without a mix)
Combine:
3 1/2 cups sugar
1/2 cup brown sugar
2 cups water
Stir until mixture boils. Cover and simmer for 10 minutes.
Add:
1 tsp. liquid maple flavoring
1/2 tsp. liquid vanilla flavoring

TORTILLA MIX

Combine:
8 cups flour
2 cups dehydrated shortening
3 Tbsp. powdered milk
1 1/2 Tbsp. salt

MINI-MIX

Combine:
1 cup flour
1/4 cup dehydrated shortening
1 tsp. powdered milk
1/2 tsp. salt

Tortillas

Combine:
1 cup Tortilla Mix (above)
1/3 cup water

Stir vigorously. Turn out on floured board and knead into a ball. Divide in thirds and roll into 6" rounds. Heat in ungreased hot pan, turning until light brown spots appear. Use for the Mexican Dinner recipe (p. 63), or for soft-shelled tacos. These are also delicious when fried until crisp in hot oil, turning once. Sprinkle with cinnamon sugar and serve for dessert.

Baked Enchiladas

Fill Tortillas with Chili, Thick and Fast (p. 62), or cooked beef or chicken. Add Picante' Sauce (p. 53) (optional) and roll up, folding the ends. Combine 2 cups prepared Tomato Sauce (p. 52) with 1 tsp. chili powder. Spread 1 cup of sauce over the bottom of a 9" x 13" baking pan. Add filled tortillas and cover with the remaining cup of Tomato Sauce. Bake at 350 degrees for 30 minutes and cover with grated cheese. Serve with lettuce, sour cream and/or guacamole.

STUFFING MIX

Combine:
1/2 cup Onion Soup Mix (p. 34)
1/2 cup dried parsley flakes
1/4 cup sage
1 Tbsp. chicken bouillon (soup base)
1/2 Tbsp. thyme (optional)

MINI-MIX

Combine:
1 Tbsp. Onion Soup Mix (p. 34)
1 Tbsp. parsley flakes
1/2 tsp. sage
1/2 tsp. chicken bouillon (soup base)
1/4 tsp. thyme (optional)

Quick and Easy Stuffing

Combine in bowl or plastic bag:
2 cups dried bread cubes (p. 41)
2 1/2 Tbsp. Stuffing Mix (above)

Shake or stir to mix evenly. Add 1/3 to 2/3 cup hot water and let sit for 5 minutes. Add 1/4 cup each: chopped celery, onions, water chestnuts (optional). If you desire tender veggies instead of crisp, microwave them first with a little water in a covered dish and then add to stuffing. Bake in covered casserole dish at 350 degrees for 15 minutes.
OR
Microwave on medium 5-10 minutes in a covered pan or dish.

Note: It is not recommended that stuffing be baked inside the turkey.

BREAD CUBES

Cut into cubes:
Day-old toast, muffins, bread, buns, etc. Dry thoroughly and store in covered container until ready to use.

Stuffed Patties Supreme
(A great way to use left-over stuffing!)

Combine:
2 lbs. lean ground hamburger or turkey burger
2 eggs and 1/2 cup milk or water
1 cup bread crumbs
2 tsp. salt
1/4 tsp. pepper

Make 16 patties, pressing mixture between 2 plates with wax paper. Place 8 patties side-by-side in large baking pan. Top each with 1/4 cup prepared stuffing (p. 40). Add 1 slice Swiss or processed cheese (optional). Cover with remaining meat patties and seal the edges. Bake patties uncovered at 400 degrees for 25 minutes.

Gravy

Combine and pour over browned meat patties:
2 1/2 cups water
1 cup White Sauce Mix (p. 54)
1 Tbsp. Onion Soup Mix (p. 34)

Cover and bake at 350 degrees with gravy for another 25 minutes until done. Remove patties and stir the gravy. Make sure you work in all of the drippings from the bottom of the pan. Serve with cooked potatoes or Onion Steamed Rice (p. 34).

Chicken with Gravy

Bake chicken pieces at 375 degrees for 45 minutes in sprayed baking pan. Make gravy (see above) and bake for another 20 minutes.

BASIC MIXES

SAUCES AND SPICE MIXES

Baking Spice Mix	p. 43
Barbecue Sauce Mix	p. 44
Catalina Dressing Mix	p. 45
Cheese Sauce Mix	p. 46
Country Gravy Mix	p. 47
French Dressing Mix	p. 48
Italian Spice Mix	p. 49
Salad Dressing Mix	p. 51
Thousand Island Dressing	p. 51
Tomato Sauce Mix	p. 52
Picante' Sauce	p. 53
Veggie Salt Mix	p. 49
White Sauce Mix	p. 54

BAKING SPICE MIX

Combine:
8 Tbsp. cinnamon
2 Tbsp. nutmeg
1 Tbsp. allspice
1 tsp. cloves (optional)

MINI-MIX

Combine:
1 tsp. cinnamon
1/4 tsp. nutmeg
1/8 tsp. allspice
pinch of cloves (optional)

SEASONED SALT MIX

Combine:
2 cups salt
3/4 cup sugar
1/4 cup dehydrated cheese
1/4 cup taco seasoning
3 Tbsp. onion powder
1 Tbsp. garlic powder
1 Tbsp. thyme
1 Tbsp. paprika

MINI-MIX

Combine:
1/2 cup salt
3 Tbsp. sugar
1 Tbsp. dehydrated cheese
1 Tbsp. taco seasoning
2 tsp. onion powder
1 tsp. garlic powder
1 tsp. thyme
1 tsp. paprika

BARBECUE SAUCE MIX

Combine:
1 1/4 cups sugar
1 1/4 cups tomato powder
1/3 cup onion powder
1 1/2 tsp. dry mustard
1 1/4 tsp. garlic powder
1/2 tsp. cloves
1/8 tsp. cinnamon

MINI-MIX

Combine:
2 Tbsp. sugar
2 Tbsp. tomato powder
1 1/2 rounded tsp. onion powder
1/4 tsp. dry mustard
1/8 tsp. garlic powder
1/16 tsp. cloves
pinch of cinnamon

Barbecue Sauce

Combine:
1/4 cup Barbecue Sauce Mix (above)
1/4 cup Tomato Sauce Mix (p. 52)

Add to:
1 cup BOILING water
1/2 Tbsp. cider vinegar

Stir until thick.

Note: This recipe is mild enough to substitute for ketchup.

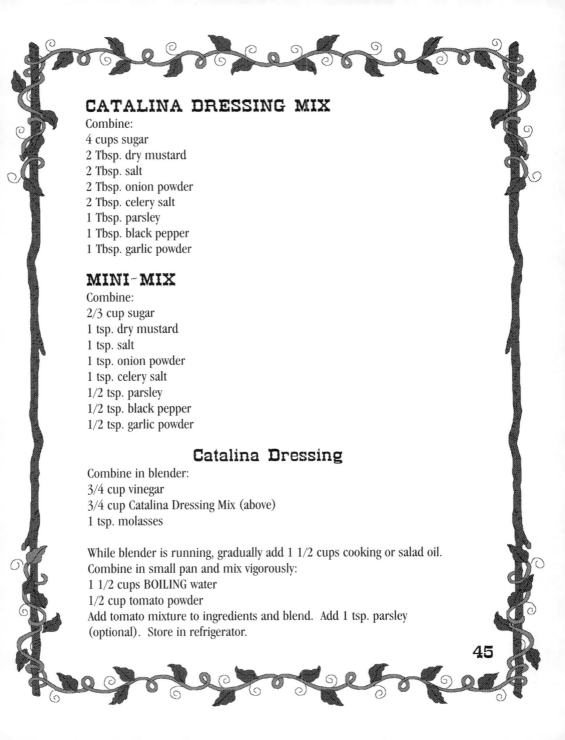

CATALINA DRESSING MIX

Combine:
4 cups sugar
2 Tbsp. dry mustard
2 Tbsp. salt
2 Tbsp. onion powder
2 Tbsp. celery salt
1 Tbsp. parsley
1 Tbsp. black pepper
1 Tbsp. garlic powder

MINI-MIX

Combine:
2/3 cup sugar
1 tsp. dry mustard
1 tsp. salt
1 tsp. onion powder
1 tsp. celery salt
1/2 tsp. parsley
1/2 tsp. black pepper
1/2 tsp. garlic powder

Catalina Dressing

Combine in blender:
3/4 cup vinegar
3/4 cup Catalina Dressing Mix (above)
1 tsp. molasses

While blender is running, gradually add 1 1/2 cups cooking or salad oil.
Combine in small pan and mix vigorously:
1 1/2 cups BOILING water
1/2 cup tomato powder
Add tomato mixture to ingredients and blend. Add 1 tsp. parsley
(optional). Store in refrigerator.

CHEESE SAUCE MIX

Combine:

4 1/2 cups dehydrated cheese

2 2/3 cups powdered milk

2 2/3 cups dehydrated butter or margarine

2 2/3 cups flour

2 tsp. onion powder

MINI-MIX

Combine:

1/3 cup dehydrated cheese powder

3 Tbsp. powdered milk

3 Tbsp. dehydrated butter or margarine

3 Tbsp. flour

1/8 tsp. onion powder

Cheese Sauce

Combine:

1 cup hot tap water

1/2 cup Cheese Sauce Mix (above)

Bring to a boil, stirring with a wire whisk (it only takes a minute!). For a
touch of color, add a few parsley flakes (optional). Use this sauce for:
Nacho chips, macaroni and cheese, cheese and broccoli, toppings for a
potato bar, or any favorite cheese sauce recipe.

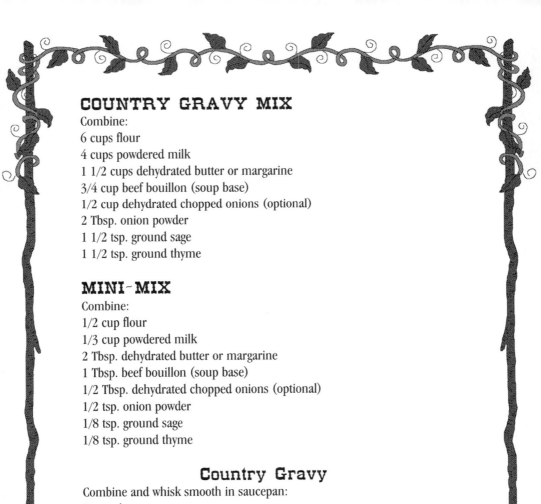

COUNTRY GRAVY MIX

Combine:

6 cups flour

4 cups powdered milk

1 1/2 cups dehydrated butter or margarine

3/4 cup beef bouillon (soup base)

1/2 cup dehydrated chopped onions (optional)

2 Tbsp. onion powder

1 1/2 tsp. ground sage

1 1/2 tsp. ground thyme

MINI-MIX

Combine:

1/2 cup flour

1/3 cup powdered milk

2 Tbsp. dehydrated butter or margarine

1 Tbsp. beef bouillon (soup base)

1/2 Tbsp. dehydrated chopped onions (optional)

1/2 tsp. onion powder

1/8 tsp. ground sage

1/8 tsp. ground thyme

Country Gravy

Combine and whisk smooth in saucepan:

3 cups hot water

1 cup Country Gravy Mix (above)

Bring to a boil, stirring constantly, until thickened (It cooks up fast!)
Add more water, if necessary, for desired consistency. This is great over
chicken-fried steaks or combined with crumble-fried hamburger,
chunks of leftover turkey or chicken. Serve on biscuits, potatoes or rice.

47

FRENCH DRESSING MIX
Combine:
1 1/2 cups sugar
1/2 cup dehydrated cheese
1-2 Tbsp. dry mustard
1 Tbsp. salt
1 Tbsp. paprika
1 Tbsp. onion powder
1 Tbsp. celery salt
1/2 to 1 tsp. black pepper
1/2 to 1 tsp. garlic powder

MINI-MIX
Combine:
1/2 cup sugar
3 Tbsp. dehydrated cheese
1-2 tsp. dry mustard
1 tsp. salt
1 tsp. paprika
1 tsp. onion powder
1 tsp. celery salt
1/4 tsp. black pepper
1/4 tsp. garlic powder

French Creamy Dressing
Mix in a blender:
3/4 cup vinegar
1/4 cup water
3/4 cup French Dressing Mix (above)
1 tsp. molasses (optional)

While blender is running, GRADUALLY add 1 1/2 cups cooking or salad oil.

Combine in a small pan and mix vigorously:
3/4 cup BOILING water
1/4 cup Tomato Sauce Mix (p. 52)
OR
Use one cup tomato paste or ketchup

Add tomato mixture to blender and mix just until blended. Store in the refrigerator.

Note: To reduce fat, may substitute 1 1/2 cups canned applesauce or reconstituted dehydrated applesauce for the oil.

ITALIAN SPICE MIX

Combine:

1/4 cup crushed basil leaf
1/4 cup ground oregano
2 Tbsp. garlic powder
1/2 cup parsley

MINI-MIX

Combine:

1/8 tsp. crushed basil leaf
1/8 tsp. ground oregano
1/16 tsp. garlic powder
1/4 tsp. parsley

This can be used in any recipe calling for Italian Seasoning.

VEGGIE SALT MIX

Combine:

1/2 cup vegetable powder*
1/4 cup salt
1 1/2 Tbsp. dill weed (optional)

MINI-MIX

Combine:

2 Tbsp. vegetable powder*
1 Tbsp. salt
1 tsp. dill weed (optional)
Combine powder, salt and dill and use in a salt shaker.

*Vegetable powder: Put 1/2 cup dehydrated vegetable stew in a blender and process until fine. Pour into a strainer and shake to separate vegetable powder from the large pieces remaining.

49

RANCH DRESSING MIX
Combine:
1 cup powdered milk or powdered buttermilk
6 Tbsp. onion powder
3 Tbsp garlic powder
3 Tbsp. parsley (crushed)
1 1/2 Tbsp. beef bouillon (soup base)
1 1/2 Tbsp. chicken bouillon (soup base)
1 1/2 Tbsp. black pepper
1 1/2 Tbsp. celery seed
1 1/2 Tbsp. dehydrated cheese

MINI-MIX
Combine:
2 1/2 Tbsp. powdered milk or powdered buttermilk
1 Tbsp. onion powder
1 1/2 tsp. garlic powder
1 1/2 tsp. crushed parsley
1 tsp. beef bouillon (soup base)
1 tsp. chicken bouillon (soup base)
1 tsp. black pepper
1 tsp. celery seed
1 tsp. dehydrated cheese

Ranch Dressing
Combine:
1 cup fat-free sour cream
1-2 Tbsp. skim milk
1-2 Tbsp. vinegar
3 Tbsp. Ranch Dressing Mix (above)

Ranch Dressing Deluxe
Combine:
1 cup salad dressing, mayonnaise, or sour cream
1/4 cup fresh buttermilk
1/2 cup cottage cheese
1/3 cup Ranch Dressing Mix (above)
1-2 Tbsp. vinegar

Tastes great on baked potatoes! Flavor improves with refrigeration.

SALAD DRESSING MIX

Combine:
3 cups sugar
1 1/2 cups powdered milk or buttermilk
1 1/2 cups powdered cheese
1/4 cup onion powder
2 Tbsp. dry mustard
2 Tbsp. salt
2 Tbsp. garlic powder
2 Tbsp. celery salt
1 Tbsp. pepper

MINI-MIX

Combine:
1/2 cup sugar
1/4 cup each powdered milk or buttermilk
1/4 cup powdered cheese
2 tsp. onion powder
1 tsp. dry mustard
1 tsp. salt
1 tsp. garlic powder
1 tsp. celery salt
1/2 tsp. pepper

Salad Dressing

Combine in a blender:
1/2 cup Salad Dressing Mix (above)
1/2 cup water and 1/3 cup vinegar

While blender is running, GRADUALLY add 3/4 cup oil.

House Dressing

Make Salad Dressing (above). Thin as desired, and add poppy seeds.

Thousand Island Dressing

Make Salad Dressing (above)
Add:
1/2 cup prepared Barbecue Sauce (p. 44)
1 grated boiled egg, and approximately 1 Tablespoon chopped sweet pickles. Thin with sweet pickle juice to desired consistency.

TOMATO SAUCE MIX

Combine:

6 3/4 cups tomato powder

1 1/2 cups dehydrated cheese

1 1/8 cups sugar

3/4 cup beef bouillon (soup base)

3/4 cup cornstarch

MINI-MIX

Combine:

3 Tbsp. tomato powder

2 tsp. dehydrated cheese

1 1/2 tsp. sugar

1 tsp. beef bouillon (soup base)

1 tsp. cornstarch

Tomato Sauce

1 scant cup BOILING water

1/4 cup Tomato Sauce Mix (above)

Important: Add Tomato Sauce Mix all at once to the boiling water. The water must be boiling or the sauce will not thicken. Remove from heat and stir vigorously with a wire whisk. Makes approximately 1 cup.

Italian Tomato Sauce

Add 1/2 tsp. Italian Spice Mix (p. 49) to 1 cup boiling water. Add 1/4 cup Tomato Sauce Mix (above) and stir vigorously. Use for Pizza and as a dip for breadsticks.

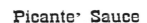

Picante' Sauce

Combine and bring to boil for one minute:
2 cups water
1/2 cup chopped green pepper
1/4 cup chopped onion

Stir 1/2 cup Tomato Sauce Mix (p. 52) into boiling mixture.

Remove from heat and add:
1 small can chopped green chilies and juice
1 cup drained stewed or fresh chopped tomatoes
Add a little Tabasco if you like it hot.

Picante' Nacho Sauce

Combine:
1 cup hot water
1/2 cup Cheese Sauce Mix (p. 46)

Cook until thick and add 1 cup Picante' Sauce (above). While hot, add
1/2-1 cup sour cream (optional). Serve over chips with lettuce topping.

Bean Dip

Cook any dried beans (pinto or chili beans are preferred). Mash them
as you would for refried beans. Add Picante' Sauce or Picante' Nacho
Sauce to desired consistency.

WHITE SAUCE MIX

Combine:
4 cups powdered milk
4 cups flour
4 cups dehydrated margarine or butter
2 tsp. salt

MINI-MIX

1/4 cup powdered milk
1/4 cup flour
1/4 cup dehydrated margarine or butter
1/8 tsp. salt

Basic White Sauce

Combine in a sauce pan:
1/2 cup White Sauce Mix (above)
1 cup hot tap water
salt and pepper as desired

Bring to boil in sauce pan. With wire whisk stir constantly over medium heat until thick to prevent scorching.

Use White Sauce Mix for:
Creamed soups and chowders, scalloped potatoes, white gravy, Creamed Vegetables (p. 55) and chicken a la king. To extend canned creamed soups as a delicious casserole base, use 2 parts Basic White Sauce to 1 part cream of chicken, mushroom, or celery soup.

Creamed Vegetables

Soak 1/2 cup dehydrated vegetables for 20 minutes in 2 cups water. Add 1 Tbsp. Onion Soup Mix (p. 34). Simmer for 20 minutes or until vegetables are tender

OR

Steam 1 cup fresh vegetables to desired consistency. Any canned vegetables also work well. Drain water from cooked vegetables. Add enough hot water to make 1 1/2 cups liquid. Stir in 3/4 cup White Sauce Mix (p. 54). Cook until thick, stirring constantly. Combine cooked vegetables and sauce, stirring gently. Serve over baked or mashed potatoes, rice or toast. Garnish with sliced boiled egg, bacon bits or crumble fried bacon, if desired.

Creamy Casseroles

Prepare creamed vegetables from above recipe using these proportions:
3 cups total liquid and 1 1/2 cups White Sauce Mix (p. 54)
Add:
2 cups cooked chicken, turkey pieces or diced ham
1 cup Onion Steamed Rice (p. 34) or cooked noodles
Cover with grated cheese and bake until cheese has melted.

Cheesy Creamed Vegetables

Substitute Cheese Sauce Mix (p. 46) in place of the White Sauce Mix.

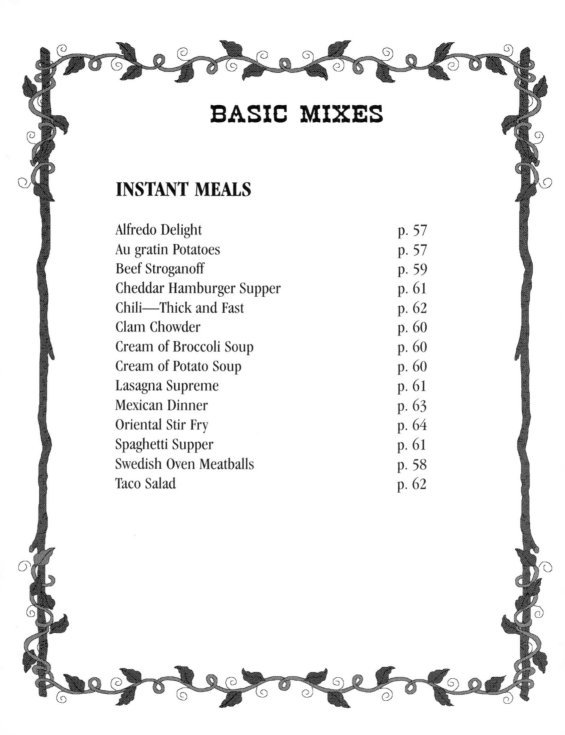

BASIC MIXES

INSTANT MEALS

Alfredo Delight	p. 57
Au gratin Potatoes	p. 57
Beef Stroganoff	p. 59
Cheddar Hamburger Supper	p. 61
Chili—Thick and Fast	p. 62
Clam Chowder	p. 60
Cream of Broccoli Soup	p. 60
Cream of Potato Soup	p. 60
Lasagna Supreme	p. 61
Mexican Dinner	p. 63
Oriental Stir Fry	p. 64
Spaghetti Supper	p. 61
Swedish Oven Meatballs	p. 58
Taco Salad	p. 62

Alfredo Delight

Add: 6 oz. linguine noodles to two quarts boiling water.
Cook 8-10 minutes until desired tenderness and drain.

In a large saucepan, combine with a wire whisk:
2 1/4 cups water
1 cup White Sauce Mix (p. 54)
1/4 cup dehydrated mushrooms (optional)
1 Tbsp. Onion Soup Mix (p. 34)
1 tsp. dried parsley

Bring to a boil, stirring constantly with a wire whisk. Pour over hot, cooked noodles. Sprinkle liberally with Parmesan cheese and serve immediately.

Au gratin Potatoes

In a 4-quart casserole dish, combine with a wire whisk:
2 cups water
1 cup Cheese Sauce Mix (p. 46)
1 tsp. dried parsley (optional)
1/4 tsp. dry mustard (optional)

Add 4 fresh potatoes cut in thin slices and stir
OR
2 cups dehydrated potato slices with an additional 2 cups water.

Bake uncovered at 350 degrees for 45-60 minutes.

Scalloped Potatoes

In a 4-quart baking dish combine with a wire whisk:
4 cups hot water
1 cup White Sauce Mix (p. 54)
1 Tbsp. Onion Soup Mix (p. 44)

Add 2 cups sliced dehydrated potatoes. Cover and bake at 375 degrees
for 15 minutes, then uncovered for 15 minutes. Sprinkle generously
with grated cheese just before serving (optional).

Swedish Oven Meatballs

Combine in a bowl:
1 lb. lean ground beef
2 slices fresh bread, crumbled
1 fresh egg
1 tsp. Onion Soup Mix (p. 34)
1/8 tsp. dried minced garlic or garlic powder
1/8 tsp. black pepper

Form into 20-30 small meatballs (a cookie scoop works great!). Place
on baking sheet sprayed with pan spray. Bake at 400 degrees for 15-20
minutes until browned and cooked through.

Serve with Swedish Sauce made by combining in a large pan:
2 cups water
1 cup White Sauce Mix (p. 54)
1 Tbsp. Onion Soup Mix (p. 34)

Cook until thickened, stirring with a wire whisk. Add cooked meatballs
to sauce and drain grease from baking sheet. Add 1/2 cup water to baking sheet and stir until drippings are dissolved. Add drippings carefully
to the sauce and stir gently. Add Caramelized Onions (p. 35) (optional).
Serve with baked potatoes or spoon over rice or toast.

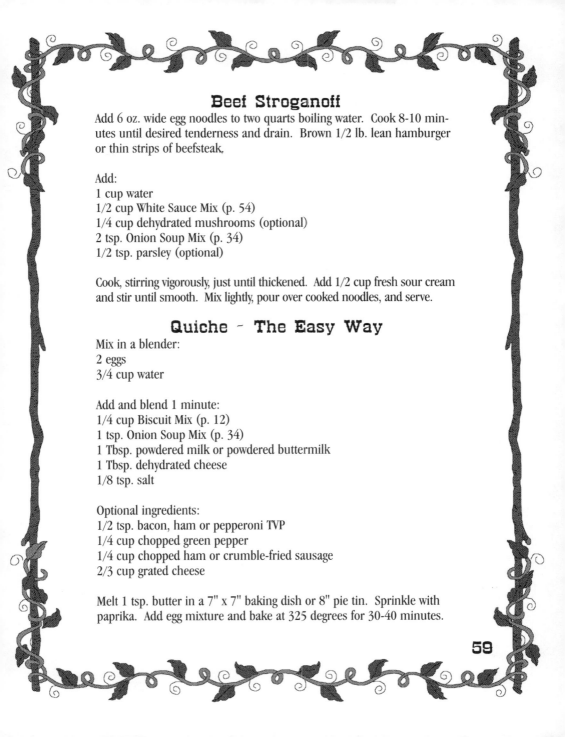

Beef Stroganoff

Add 6 oz. wide egg noodles to two quarts boiling water. Cook 8-10 minutes until desired tenderness and drain. Brown 1/2 lb. lean hamburger or thin strips of beefsteak.

Add:
1 cup water
1/2 cup White Sauce Mix (p. 54)
1/4 cup dehydrated mushrooms (optional)
2 tsp. Onion Soup Mix (p. 34)
1/2 tsp. parsley (optional)

Cook, stirring vigorously, just until thickened. Add 1/2 cup fresh sour cream and stir until smooth. Mix lightly, pour over cooked noodles, and serve.

Quiche ~ The Easy Way

Mix in a blender:
2 eggs
3/4 cup water

Add and blend 1 minute:
1/4 cup Biscuit Mix (p. 12)
1 tsp. Onion Soup Mix (p. 34)
1 Tbsp. powdered milk or powdered buttermilk
1 Tbsp. dehydrated cheese
1/8 tsp. salt

Optional ingredients:
1/2 tsp. bacon, ham or pepperoni TVP
1/4 cup chopped green pepper
1/4 cup chopped ham or crumble-fried sausage
2/3 cup grated cheese

Melt 1 tsp. butter in a 7" x 7" baking dish or 8" pie tin. Sprinkle with paprika. Add egg mixture and bake at 325 degrees for 30-40 minutes.

Cream of Broccoli Soup

Steam just until fork-tender 1 cup fresh diced broccoli
OR
Follow directions on p. 55 to cook dehydrated broccoli.
Remove broccoli and add water to stock to make 3 cups.
Add:
3/4 cup White Sauce Mix (p. 54)
Cook and stir until thickened, then add steamed broccoli.

Note: Good stock for any soup can be made by simmering celery tops
and straining broth. You may want to keep a jar in your freezer to collect all vegetable juices drained off before serving. This stock makes a
fuller-flavored and more nutritional soup.

Cream of Potato Soup

Boil 2 cups diced fresh potatoes. Drain off water when potatoes are tender or use 2 cups leftover cooked potatoes.

Add:
Stock or water to equal 4 cups liquid.
1 1/2 cups White Sauce Mix (p. 54)
Stir until slightly thickened.
Then Add:
1/4 cup chopped Caramelized Onions (p. 35)
1/4 cup each cooked carrots and celery pieces (optional)
2 cups cooked, diced potatoes
Garnish with bacon bits (TVP) (optional)

Clam Chowder

Make the above recipe and add one or two cans of clams. If you prefer a
thinner base, experiment with the amount of White Sauce Mix added.
For fuller flavor, you may prefer to add more powdered milk and butter.

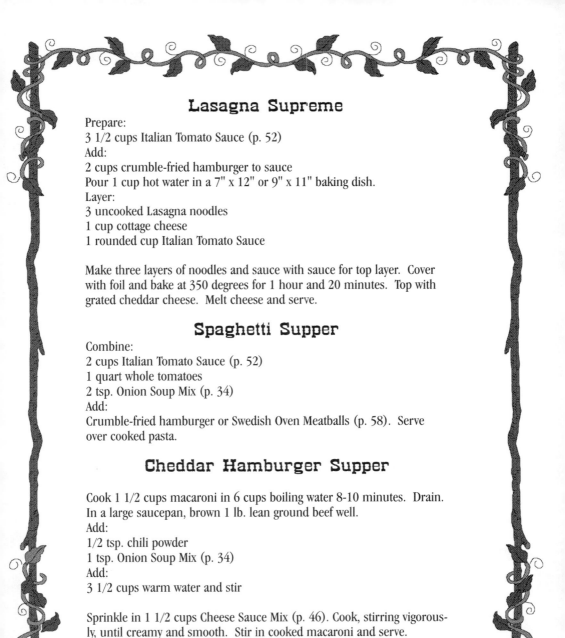

Lasagna Supreme

Prepare:
3 1/2 cups Italian Tomato Sauce (p. 52)
Add:
2 cups crumble-fried hamburger to sauce
Pour 1 cup hot water in a 7" x 12" or 9" x 11" baking dish.
Layer:
3 uncooked Lasagna noodles
1 cup cottage cheese
1 rounded cup Italian Tomato Sauce

Make three layers of noodles and sauce with sauce for top layer. Cover with foil and bake at 350 degrees for 1 hour and 20 minutes. Top with grated cheddar cheese. Melt cheese and serve.

Spaghetti Supper

Combine:
2 cups Italian Tomato Sauce (p. 52)
1 quart whole tomatoes
2 tsp. Onion Soup Mix (p. 34)
Add:
Crumble-fried hamburger or Swedish Oven Meatballs (p. 58). Serve over cooked pasta.

Cheddar Hamburger Supper

Cook 1 1/2 cups macaroni in 6 cups boiling water 8-10 minutes. Drain. In a large saucepan, brown 1 lb. lean ground beef well.
Add:
1/2 tsp. chili powder
1 tsp. Onion Soup Mix (p. 34)
Add:
3 1/2 cups warm water and stir

Sprinkle in 1 1/2 cups Cheese Sauce Mix (p. 46). Cook, stirring vigorously, until creamy and smooth. Stir in cooked macaroni and serve.

Nacho Potato Bake

In a 4-quart casserole dish, combine with wire whisk:
2 cups water
1 cup Cheese Sauce Mix (p. 46)
1/2 cup salsa or Picante' Sauce (p. 53)
Add:
4 fresh thinly-sliced potatoes and stir to cover
OR
2 cups dehydrated potato slices and 2 cups additional water.

Bake at 350 degrees for 45-60 minutes. When serving, top with extra cheese sauce or grated cheese, as desired.

Chili - Thick and Fast

Combine in a large pan:
2 cups boiling water
1 Tbsp. chili seasoning
1 Tbsp. Onion Soup Mix (p. 34)
Add:
1/2 cup Tomato Sauce Mix (p. 52)
Stir until well blended.
Add:
2 cups cooked chili beans
1 pound crumble-fried hamburger
2 cups stewed tomatoes with juice

Bring ingredients to a simmer and serve immediately or keep it hot in a crockpot.

Taco Salad

Cover corn chips with Chili – Thick and Fast (above). Top, as desired, with lettuce, grated cheese, olives and peppers. Garnish with sour cream or Dip for Chips and Veggies (p. 34).

Mexican Dinner

Combine and bring to a boil:
3 cups water
1 tsp. chili or taco seasoning
1/2 tsp. beef bouillon (soup base)
While boiling, add 1/2 cup Tomato Sauce Mix (p. 52). Dip two corn or
two Flour Tortillas (p. 39) in above sauce
OR
Dip in regular tomato sauce with chili and beef seasonings. Place side
by side in the bottom of a 9" x 13" pan (edges will overlap).
Add:
hot crumble-fried hamburger or Chili-Thick and Fast (p. 62)
olives
cheese

Repeat with two more layers of dipped tortillas and meat or chili topping.
End with meat and grated cheese. Pour remaining sauce over the top.
Cover with foil and bake at 350 degrees for 15-20 minutes until cheese
melts. Cut into squares and serve immediately. Garnish with tossed
salad and sour cream.

Mexican Dinner
(without baking)

Dip one flour tortilla in sauce (above) and place on a plate. Add toppings,
as desired. Cover with a second dipped tortilla and a second layer of
toppings. Garnish with tossed salad and sour cream. Serve immediately.

Coleslaw

Combine to make about 3 cups:
Grated cabbage, grated carrot and grated onion
Combine and boil until thickened:
1/2 cup water
2 Tbsp. white vinegar
5 Tbsp. Oriental Stir Fry Mix (p. 64). Pour sauce over grated coleslaw
and chill well before serving.

ORIENTAL STIR FRY MIX

Combine:
2 cups sugar
3/4 cup cornstarch
3 1/2 Tbsp. Onion Soup Mix (p. 34)
2 tsp. onion powder
2 tsp. garlic powder
1 tsp. ground ginger
1 tsp. black pepper

MINI-MIX

Combine:
2 1/2 Tbsp. sugar
2 tsp. cornstarch
1 tsp. Onion Soup Mix (p. 34)
1/4 tsp. onion powder
1/4 tsp. ground ginger
1/4 tsp. garlic powder
1/8 tsp. black pepper

Oriental Stir Fry

Stir fry 4-5 cups of cut, thinly-sliced fresh or frozen vegetables (cabbage, onions, green peppers, carrots, green beans, mushrooms, summer squash, broccoli, and cauliflower). Cook for 5-8 minutes or until tender.

Add:
1-2 cups steamed chicken, leftover roast beef or turkey
1/2 cup water
1 Tbsp. white vinegar
1/8 cup soy sauce

Sprinkle on 1/4 cup Oriental Stir Fry Mix (above). Stir and cook for 2-3 minutes until sauce thickens.

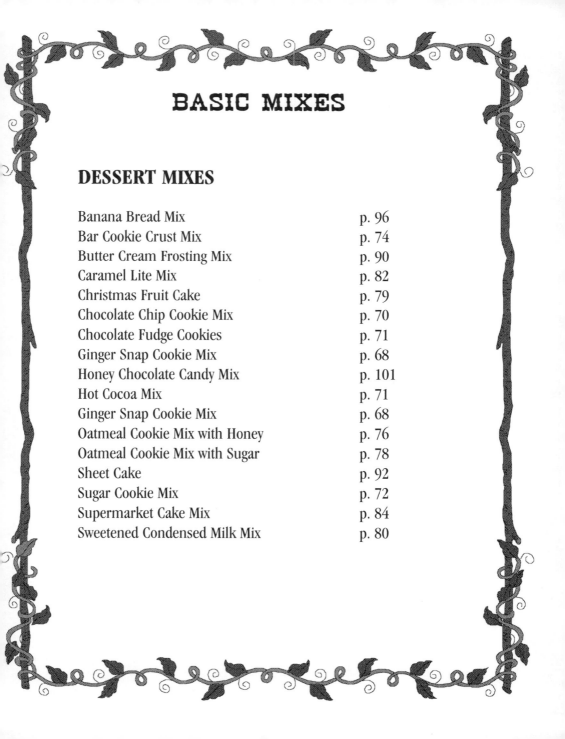

BASIC MIXES

DESSERT MIXES

Banana Bread Mix	p. 96
Bar Cookie Crust Mix	p. 74
Butter Cream Frosting Mix	p. 90
Caramel Lite Mix	p. 82
Christmas Fruit Cake	p. 79
Chocolate Chip Cookie Mix	p. 70
Chocolate Fudge Cookies	p. 71
Ginger Snap Cookie Mix	p. 68
Honey Chocolate Candy Mix	p. 101
Hot Cocoa Mix	p. 71
Ginger Snap Cookie Mix	p. 68
Oatmeal Cookie Mix with Honey	p. 76
Oatmeal Cookie Mix with Sugar	p. 78
Sheet Cake	p. 92
Sugar Cookie Mix	p. 72
Supermarket Cake Mix	p. 84
Sweetened Condensed Milk Mix	p. 80

BASIC COOKIE MIX

Combine:

6 cups flour
1 3/4 cups white sugar
1 1/2 cups brown sugar
1 cup dehydrated margarine or shortening
3 Tbsp. dehydrated whole eggs
2 tsp. salt
1 1/4 tsp. baking soda

MINI-MIX

Combine:

1 cup flour
1/3 cup white sugar
1/4 cup brown sugar
3 Tbsp. dehydrated margarine or shortening
1/2 Tbsp. dehydrated whole egg
1/4 tsp. salt
1/8 tsp. baking soda

Pineapple Macaroons

Combine:

1 1/2 cups Basic Cookie Mix (above)
2/3 cup shredded coconut
1/2 cup crushed pineapple with juice
1/2 cup chopped nuts

Mixture seems dry at first. Continue stirring until all ingredients are moist. Drop dough by teaspoonful onto lightly greased baking sheets. Bake at 350 degrees for 12-15 minutes until edges are golden brown. Glaze while hot with Lemon Butter Cream Glaze Mix (p. 91).

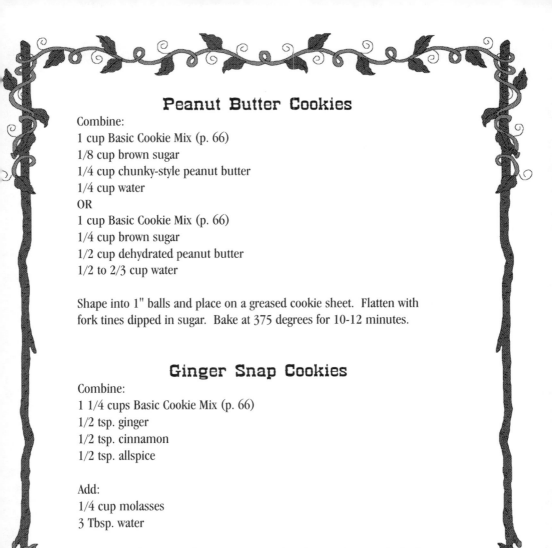

Peanut Butter Cookies

Combine:
1 cup Basic Cookie Mix (p. 66)
1/8 cup brown sugar
1/4 cup chunky-style peanut butter
1/4 cup water
OR
1 cup Basic Cookie Mix (p. 66)
1/4 cup brown sugar
1/2 cup dehydrated peanut butter
1/2 to 2/3 cup water

Shape into 1" balls and place on a greased cookie sheet. Flatten with
fork tines dipped in sugar. Bake at 375 degrees for 10-12 minutes.

Ginger Snap Cookies

Combine:
1 1/4 cups Basic Cookie Mix (p. 66)
1/2 tsp. ginger
1/2 tsp. cinnamon
1/2 tsp. allspice

Add:
1/4 cup molasses
3 Tbsp. water

Drop by half teaspoonsful on greased cookie sheet. Flatten with the bottom of a glass dipped in sugar. Bake at 350 degrees for 10-12 minutes.

Note: If you are a Ginger Snap lover, you may want the convenience of
the Ginger Snap Cookie Mix found on page 68.

GINGER SNAP COOKIE MIX

Combine:

6 cups flour
1 3/4 cups white sugar
1 1/2 cups brown sugar
1 cup dehydrated margarine or shortening
3 Tbsp. dehydrated whole egg
1 heaping Tbsp. ginger
1 heaping Tbsp. cinnamon
1 heaping Tbsp. allspice
2 tsp. salt
1 1/4 tsp. baking soda

MINI-MIX

Combine:

1 cup flour
1/3 cup white sugar
1/4 cup brown sugar
3 Tbsp. dehydrated margarine or shortening
1/2 Tbsp. dehydrated whole egg
1/2 tsp. ginger
1/2 tsp. cinnamon
1/2 tsp. allspice
1/4 tsp. salt
1/8 tsp. baking soda

Ginger Snap Cookies

Combine:

1 1/4 cup Ginger Snap Cookie Mix (above)
1/4 cup molasses
1/4 cup water

Drop by half teaspoonsful on a greased cookie sheet. Flatten with the bottom of a glass dipped in sugar. Bake at 350 degrees for 12-15 minutes.

CRUMBLE TOPPING MIX

Combine:

2 cups brown sugar

1 cup chopped nuts

3/4 cup dehydrated margarine or butter

1/2 cup Biscuit Mix (p. 12)

1 1/2 Tbsp. cinnamon

MINI-MIX

Combine:

1/2 cup brown sugar

1/4 cup chopped nuts

3 Tbsp. dehydrated margarine or butter

2 Tbsp. Biscuit Mix (p. 12)

1 tsp. cinnamon

Use with the following recipes:

Breakfast Cake	p. 19
Fruit Breakfast Pizza	p. 14
Muffins	p. 32
Cinnamon Rolls	p. 27
Heavenly Orange Rolls	p. 27

Note: The butter in this topping mix gives it a rich taste and it browns well. Use it generously as a topping for an added touch of flavor to cookies and other baked desserts.

CHOCOLATE CHIP COOKIE MIX
Combine:
5 1/3 cups flour
1 1/3 cups ground oatmeal*
2 cups brown sugar
2 cups white sugar
2 cups dehydrated margarine
1/4 cup dehydrated whole eggs
2 tsp. baking powder
2 tsp. baking soda
1 tsp. salt
1/2 tsp. powdered vanilla

MINI-MIX
Combine:
1 1/3 cups flour
1/3 cup ground oatmeal*
1/2 cup brown sugar
1/2 cup white sugar
1/2 cup dehydrated margarine
1 Tbsp. dehydrated whole eggs
1/2 tsp. baking powder
1/2 tsp. baking soda
1/4 tsp. salt
1/16 tsp. powdered vanilla

Chocolate Chip Cookies
Combine:
2 cups Chocolate Chip Cookie Mix (above)
1/3 cup water
1/2 cup chocolate chips
1/4 cup chopped nuts

Drop by teaspoonful or cookie scoop on sprayed or greased sheet. For crisper cookies, flatten with a glass dipped in sugar before baking. Bake at 375 degrees for 10-12 minutes.

Note: Ground oatmeal flour keeps the cookie moist and improves the texture. Rolled oats can be ground in a wheat grinder or ground in a blender.

Chocolate Fudge Cookies

Combine:
2 cups Chocolate Chip Cookie Mix (p. 70)
1/4 cup cooking cocoa
1/2 cup chocolate chips
1/4 cup chopped nuts
Add:
1/3 cup water

Drop by teaspoonsful on a sprayed or greased cookie sheet. Bake at 375 degrees for 10-12 minutes.

HOT COCOA MIX

Combine:
4 1/2 cups regular powdered milk or 9 cups instant powdered milk
1 cup sugar
1/2 cup cocoa

MINI-MIX

Combine:
2 Tbsp. regular powdered milk or 1/4 cup instant powdered milk
1/2 tsp. cocoa
1 tsp. sugar

Hot Chocolate

Combine in quart jar, cover and shake hard, or mix on low in a blender:
1/3 cup Hot Cocoa Mix made with regular milk, or
2/3 cup Hot Cocoa Mix made with instant milk
1 cup hottest tap water

Note: This mix has no thickeners or preservatives and it tastes better than commercial cocoa mixes!

71

SUGAR COOKIE MIX

Combine:

6 cups flour

3 cups sugar

1 1/2 cups dehydrated butter

1 1/2 tsp. baking powder

2 tsp. cream of tartar (a must)

1 1/2 tsp. salt

1 tsp. powdered vanilla

MINI-MIX

Combine:

2 cups flour

1 cup sugar

1/2 cup dehydrated butter

1/2 tsp. baking powder

1/2 tsp. cream of tartar (a must)

1/2 tsp. salt

1/8 tsp. powdered vanilla

Sugar Cookie Cutouts

Combine:
2 cups Sugar Cookie Mix (p. 72)
1 egg, plus enough water to equal 1/3 cup liquid

Stir liquid into mix. Form into a ball, pressing crumble mixture with
your hands. Dust board with Sugar Cookie Mix, roll out and cut. Bake
at 350 degrees on a greased cookie sheet for 10-12 minutes. Do not
overbake. Cookies should not be browned. Cool slightly and place in an
airtight container. When cool, frost with Butter Cream Frosting (p. 90).

Snickerdoodles

Combine:
2 cups Sugar Cookie Mix (p. 72)
1 beaten egg, plus enough water to equal 1/3 cup liquid
1/2 cup chopped walnuts

Stir liquid into mix and form dough into a ball with your hands. Pinch
off a small amount and roll it in a cinnamon-sugar mixture.

Cinnamon Sugar
Combine:
3 Tbsp. cinnamon
1 cup sugar

Place on a greased cookie sheet and flatten slightly with glass. Bake at 350
degrees for 12-15 minutes. Cool slightly and place in an airtight container.

BAR COOKIE CRUST MIX

Combine:
4 cups rolled oats
4 cups brown sugar
3 1/2 cups whole wheat or white flour
1 Tbsp. baking soda
1/2 Tbsp. cream of tartar
1 tsp. salt

MINI-MIX

Combine:
1 1/4 cups rolled oats
1 1/4 cups brown sugar
1 cup whole wheat or white flour
1 tsp. baking soda
1/2 tsp. cream of tartar
1/4 tsp. salt

Bar Cookies

Combine:
3 cups Bar Cookie Crust Mix (above)
1 cube (1/2 cup) softened or melted table margarine

To make the crust, flour your fingers and pat half of the crust mixture in a greased 9" x 9" square pan. Reserve the other half of the mixture as a topping crust.

Cover with a filling:
Date Bar Cookie Filling   p. 75
Mincemeat Bar Cookie Filling   p. 75
Apple Bar Cookie Filling   p. 75
Any canned pie filling works great

Crumble remaining crust mixture over the top. Bake at 350 degrees for 20 minutes. Cut in 2"-3" squares and serve hot with ice cream or whipped cream.

Date Bar Cookie Filling

Combine:

2 cups chopped dates

2 Tbsp. brown sugar

Juice of half of a lemon or 2 Tbsp. lemon concentrate

1 cup water

Combine all ingredients in a saucepan. Cook, stirring constantly, for 5 minutes. Use with Bar Cookie Crust (p. 74) in a 9" x 9" pan.

Apple Bar Cookie Filling

Combine:

3 cups cooked sliced apples

OR

3 cups thick reconstituted applesauce

1/4 cup brown sugar

1/2 tsp. cinnamon

Combine and use with Bar Cookie Crust (p. 74). Makes filling for 9" x 9" pan.

Mincemeat Bar Cookie Filling

3 cups Mincemeat (p. 79)

Drain liquid from mincemeat and use with Bar Cookie Crust (p. 74). Makes filling for 9" x 9" pan. This tastes even better the second day!

Note: Any pie filling works well with this crust!

OATMEAL COOKIE MIX WITH HONEY

Combine:

9 cups whole wheat flour

1 1/2 cups dehydrated applesauce (optional), see p. 77

1/4 cup cinnamon

2 Tbsp. baking powder

1 Tbsp. baking soda

MINI-MIX

Combine:

3 cups whole wheat flour

1/2 cup dehydrated applesauce (optional), see p. 77

4 tsp. cinnamon

2 tsp. baking powder

1 tsp. baking soda

Note: Four Oatmeal Cookie Mixes will fill a 30-pound container (a Maxi-Mix!)

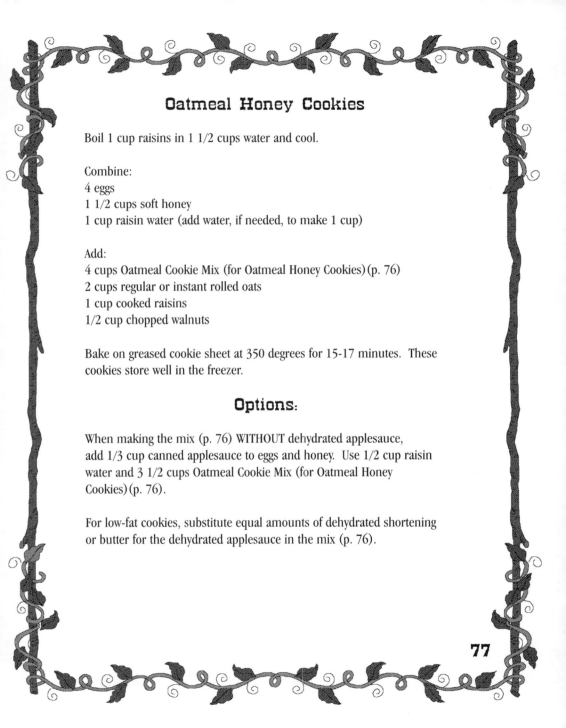

Oatmeal Honey Cookies

Boil 1 cup raisins in 1 1/2 cups water and cool.

Combine:
4 eggs
1 1/2 cups soft honey
1 cup raisin water (add water, if needed, to make 1 cup)

Add:
4 cups Oatmeal Cookie Mix (for Oatmeal Honey Cookies) (p. 76)
2 cups regular or instant rolled oats
1 cup cooked raisins
1/2 cup chopped walnuts

Bake on greased cookie sheet at 350 degrees for 15-17 minutes. These cookies store well in the freezer.

Options:

When making the mix (p. 76) WITHOUT dehydrated applesauce, add 1/3 cup canned applesauce to eggs and honey. Use 1/2 cup raisin water and 3 1/2 cups Oatmeal Cookie Mix (for Oatmeal Honey Cookies) (p. 76).

For low-fat cookies, substitute equal amounts of dehydrated shortening or butter for the dehydrated applesauce in the mix (p. 76).

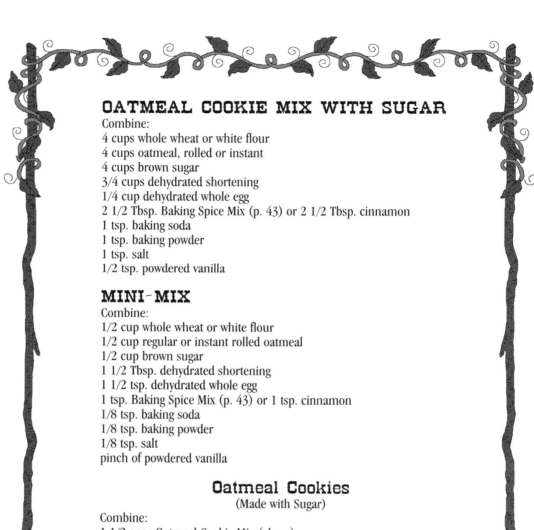

OATMEAL COOKIE MIX WITH SUGAR

Combine:

4 cups whole wheat or white flour
4 cups oatmeal, rolled or instant
4 cups brown sugar
3/4 cups dehydrated shortening
1/4 cup dehydrated whole egg
2 1/2 Tbsp. Baking Spice Mix (p. 43) or 2 1/2 Tbsp. cinnamon
1 tsp. baking soda
1 tsp. baking powder
1 tsp. salt
1/2 tsp. powdered vanilla

MINI-MIX

Combine:

1/2 cup whole wheat or white flour
1/2 cup regular or instant rolled oatmeal
1/2 cup brown sugar
1 1/2 Tbsp. dehydrated shortening
1 1/2 tsp. dehydrated whole egg
1 tsp. Baking Spice Mix (p. 43) or 1 tsp. cinnamon
1/8 tsp. baking soda
1/8 tsp. baking powder
1/8 tsp. salt
pinch of powdered vanilla

Oatmeal Cookies
(Made with Sugar)

Combine:

1 1/2 cups Oatmeal Cookie Mix (above)
1/2 cup water
3/4 cup raisins or chocolate chips
1/3 cup chopped nuts

Drop by teaspoonful or cookie scoop onto a greased cookie sheet.
Flatten with a glass dipped in cinnamon sugar (p. 73). Bake at 350
degrees for 15 minutes.

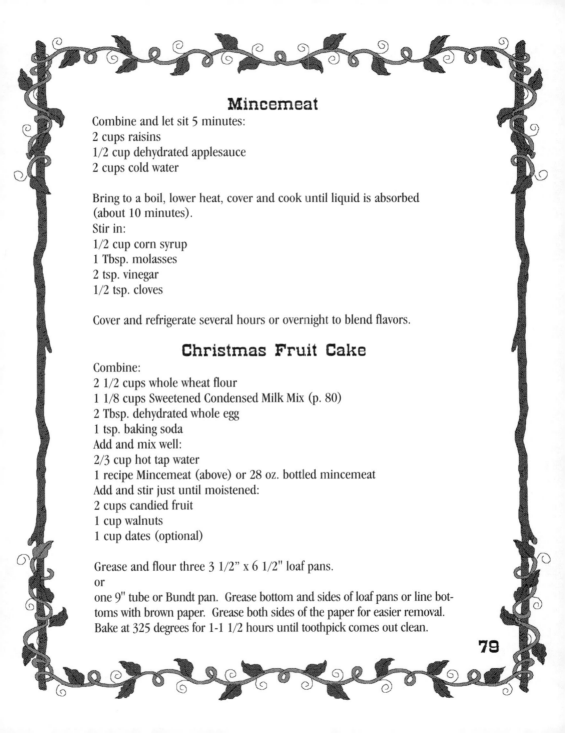

Mincemeat

Combine and let sit 5 minutes:
2 cups raisins
1/2 cup dehydrated applesauce
2 cups cold water

Bring to a boil, lower heat, cover and cook until liquid is absorbed
(about 10 minutes).
Stir in:
1/2 cup corn syrup
1 Tbsp. molasses
2 tsp. vinegar
1/2 tsp. cloves

Cover and refrigerate several hours or overnight to blend flavors.

Christmas Fruit Cake

Combine:
2 1/2 cups whole wheat flour
1 1/8 cups Sweetened Condensed Milk Mix (p. 80)
2 Tbsp. dehydrated whole egg
1 tsp. baking soda
Add and mix well:
2/3 cup hot tap water
1 recipe Mincemeat (above) or 28 oz. bottled mincemeat
Add and stir just until moistened:
2 cups candied fruit
1 cup walnuts
1 cup dates (optional)

Grease and flour three 3 1/2" x 6 1/2" loaf pans.
or
one 9" tube or Bundt pan. Grease bottom and sides of loaf pans or line bot-
toms with brown paper. Grease both sides of the paper for easier removal.
Bake at 325 degrees for 1-1 1/2 hours until toothpick comes out clean.

SWEETENED CONDENSED MILK MIX
Combine:
6 cups sugar
1 1/2 cups dehydrated margarine or butter
6 cups powdered milk

MINI-MIX
Combine:
1/2 cup sugar
1/8 cup dehydrated margarine or butter
1/2 cup powdered milk

This recipe works equally well with either instant
or regular powdered milk!

Sweetened Condensed Milk
(may be used with any sweetened condensed milk recipe)

Start with 1/4 cup very hot water in a blender. While blender is running,
gradually add 1 1/8 cups Sweetened Condensed Milk Mix (above).
Process until smooth. Makes 14 oz.

Swedish Rice Pudding

Combine:
1/2 cup prepared Sweetened Condensed Milk (p. 80)
1 1/2 to 2 cups hot cooked rice

Garnish with 1/2-1 tsp. cinnamon sugar (p. 73). Serve with milk, whipped cream or ice cream.

Lemon Cream Cheese Pie

Prepare 1 full recipe Bar Cookie Crust Mix (p. 74) for pie crust. Stir and pat out all of crust mixture into a greased 9" x 13" pan. Bake at 350 degrees for 6-8 minutes.

Filling:
Beat one 8-oz. package cream cheese until light and fluffy.

Combine in sauce pan:
1/3 cup boiling water
1/3 cup lemon juice
1/2 tsp. powdered vanilla

Add and Mix:
2 1/4 cups Sweetened Condensed Milk Mix (p. 80).

Combine:
COOLED lemon mixture with whipped cream cheese. Beat mixture until creamy and smooth. Fold in 2 cups whipped cream or non-dairy substitute.

Spread lemon cheese pie filling over COOLED prepared crust. Refrigerate 2-3 hours. Top with cherry pie filling. Sprinkle with slivered almonds.

Caramel Popcorn

Mix together in a pan:
1 cup corn syrup
1/2 cup boiling water

Stir until corn syrup dissolves.

Add to boiling liquid:
1 1/8 cups Sweetened Condensed Milk Mix (p. 80)
2 cups brown sugar
1/2 cup dehydrated butter or margarine
1/4 tsp. powdered vanilla

Lower heat and cook to soft ball stage (234-238 degrees) (it cooks up fast!). Pour hot mixture over 1 gallon popped popcorn. Add peanuts and serve like Cracker Jacks or make into popcorn balls.

CARAMEL LITE MIX
4 cups brown sugar
2 2/3 cups dehydrated margarine or butter
4 cups powdered milk
1/4 tsp. powdered vanilla

MINI-MIX
1/2 cup brown sugar
1/2 cup dehydrated margarine or butter
1/3 cup powdered milk
pinch of powdered vanilla

Use this caramel mix with the recipes on page 83.

Caramel Lite Sauce

(Great as an ice cream topping or for popcorn treats)

Mix together and bring to a boil:
1/2 cup corn syrup or light clover honey
1/4 cup hot water

Add 1 1/3 cups Caramel Lite Mix (p. 82) to boiling liquid. Lower heat and cook until mixture reaches soft ball stage (234-238 degrees).

Note: If sauce gets too thick in the refrigerator, add a little hot water before serving.

Caramel Honey Popcorn Balls

Make Caramel Lite Sauce (above).
Add chopped pecans or roasted peanuts (optional).
Pour hot caramel sauce over 1 gallon popped popcorn. With buttered hands, form mixture into popcorn balls.

Caramel Honey Popcorn Cake

Follow above recipe and press into a buttered tube or bundt pan. Turn out immediately onto a plate. Decorate top with sliced gumdrops or other candies. Slice to serve.

SUPERMARKET CAKE MIX

Combine:

7 cups flour
5 1/4 cups sugar
1 3/4 cups dehydrated shortening
1/3 rounded cup powdered milk
3 Tbsp. baking powder
2 1/2 tsp. powdered vanilla
2 scant tsp. salt

MINI-MIX

Combine:

1 cup flour
3/4 cup sugar
1/4 cup dehydrated shortening
1 Tbsp. powdered milk
1 1/4 tsp. baking powder
1/4 tsp. powdered vanilla
1/4 tsp. salt

Note: If fresh eggs are not available, for each cup of mix, add 1 Tbsp. dehydrated whole egg or dehydrated egg white, plus 3 additional Tbsp. water to each recipe.

Use this mix for the following recipes:

Yellow Cake	Marble Cake
Orange Cake	Chocolate Cake
Applesauce Spice Cake	Sponge Cake or Shortcake

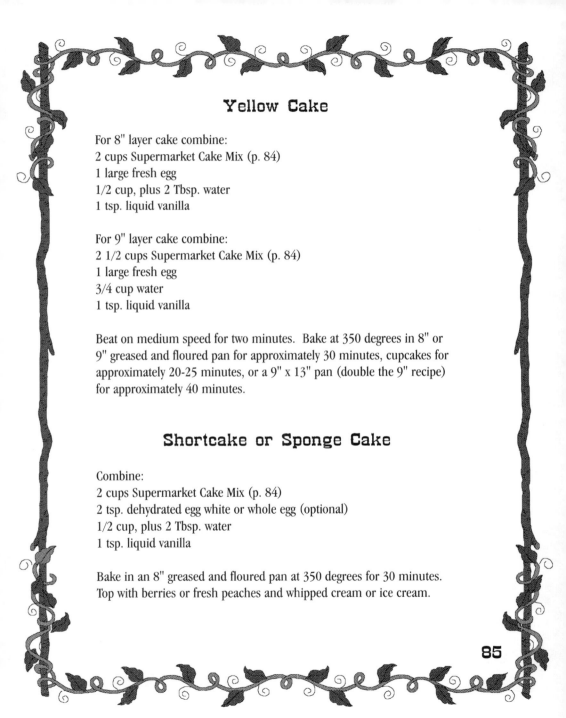

Yellow Cake

For 8" layer cake combine:
2 cups Supermarket Cake Mix (p. 84)
1 large fresh egg
1/2 cup, plus 2 Tbsp. water
1 tsp. liquid vanilla

For 9" layer cake combine:
2 1/2 cups Supermarket Cake Mix (p. 84)
1 large fresh egg
3/4 cup water
1 tsp. liquid vanilla

Beat on medium speed for two minutes. Bake at 350 degrees in 8" or 9" greased and floured pan for approximately 30 minutes, cupcakes for approximately 20-25 minutes, or a 9" x 13" pan (double the 9" recipe) for approximately 40 minutes.

Shortcake or Sponge Cake

Combine:
2 cups Supermarket Cake Mix (p. 84)
2 tsp. dehydrated egg white or whole egg (optional)
1/2 cup, plus 2 Tbsp. water
1 tsp. liquid vanilla

Bake in an 8" greased and floured pan at 350 degrees for 30 minutes. Top with berries or fresh peaches and whipped cream or ice cream.

Marble Cake

Prepare an 8" or 9" Yellow Cake (p. 85). Pour all but half cup of the batter into greased and floured cake pan. Add 2 Tbsp. cocoa to remaining batter and mix well. Drop chocolate batter by teaspoonsful onto the Yellow Cake batter. Cut through batter with 2-3 long strokes with a knife. Bake at 350 degrees for approximately 30 minutes.

Orange Cake

Mix batter according to directions for an 8" or 9" Yellow Cake (p. 85).

Add:
1/2 tsp. grated orange peel or dehydrated orange peel.

Tip: If you grate and freeze lemon and orange peelings as you use the fruit, it's very convenient when cooking!

Add:
1/2 tsp. powdered orange flavoring

Bake at 350 degrees for approximately 30 minutes. Frost with Orange Butter Cream Frosting (p. 91).

Applesauce Spice Cake

Combine in bowl and let sit for 3-5 minutes:
1/4 cup dehydrated applesauce
1 cup water
Add:
1 egg
2 cups Supermarket Cake Mix (p. 84)
1/3 cup raisins
2 scant tsp. Baking Spice Mix (p. 43)

Bake at 350 degrees in a 9" x 9" pan for 35-40 minutes. Cool and frost with Banana Butter Cream Frosting (p. 91).

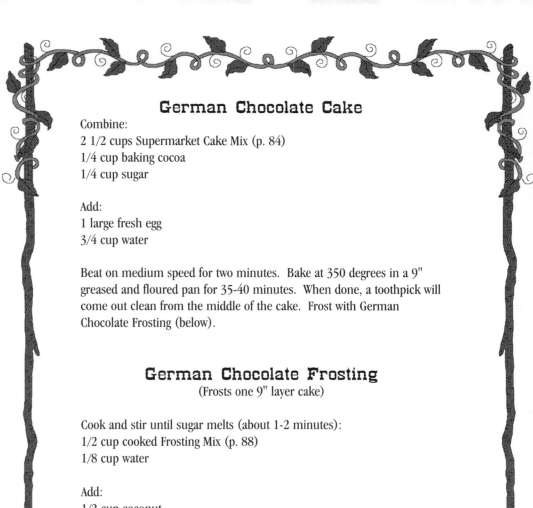

German Chocolate Cake

Combine:
2 1/2 cups Supermarket Cake Mix (p. 84)
1/4 cup baking cocoa
1/4 cup sugar

Add:
1 large fresh egg
3/4 cup water

Beat on medium speed for two minutes. Bake at 350 degrees in a 9"
greased and floured pan for 35-40 minutes. When done, a toothpick will
come out clean from the middle of the cake. Frost with German
Chocolate Frosting (below).

German Chocolate Frosting
(Frosts one 9" layer cake)

Cook and stir until sugar melts (about 1-2 minutes):
1/2 cup cooked Frosting Mix (p. 88)
1/8 cup water

Add:
1/2 cup coconut
1/2 cup chopped nuts

COOKED FROSTING MIX
Combine:
6 2/3 cups sugar
4 cups dehydrated butter
1/3 rounded cup cornstarch
1/3 rounded cup flour
1/2 tsp. powdered vanilla

MINI-MIX
Combine:
1/3 cup sugar
3 Tbsp. dehydrated butter
1 tsp. cornstarch
1 tsp. flour
pinch powdered vanilla

Chocolate Fudge Frosting
Combine:
1/2 cup Cooked Frosting Mix (above)
1 Tbsp. cocoa
1/8 cup water

Cook and stir for about a minute.

Stir in:
1/4 cup powdered sugar.

DEVILS FOOD WHOLE WHEAT CAKE MIX

Combine:
6 cups whole wheat flour
4 cups sugar
1 1/2 cups baking cocoa
1 1/4 cups dehydrated shortening
1/4 cup powdered milk
1/4 cup dehydrated whole eggs
2 Tbsp. baking soda
2 1/2 tsp. powdered vanilla
1 1/2 tsp. salt

MINI-MIX

Combine:
1 1/2 cups whole wheat flour
1 cup sugar
1/3 cup baking cocoa
1/4 cup dehydrated shortening
2 Tbsp. powdered milk
2 Tbsp. dehydrated whole eggs
1 1/2 tsp. baking soda
1/4 tsp. powdered vanilla
1/8 tsp. salt

Devils Food Whole Wheat Cake

Combine:
2 1/2 cups Devils Food Whole Wheat Cake Mix (above)
1 1/4 cups water

Beat two minutes. Bake at 350 degrees in a greased and floured 9" pan for 35 minutes.

Note: For a special taste and texture, try:
2 1/2 cups Devils Food Whole Wheat Cake Mix (above)
3/4 cup water
1/2 cup buttermilk

Bake in a greased and floured 9" cake pan at 350 degrees for 40 minutes.

89

BUTTER CREAM FROSTING MIX

Combine:

8 cups powdered sugar

1 1/2 cups dehydrated margarine or butter

1 cup cornstarch

1/2 tsp. powdered vanilla

MINI-MIX

Combine:

2 cups powdered sugar

1/3 cup margarine or butter

1/4 cup cornstarch

pinch powdered vanilla

Butter Cream Frosting
(for 9" layer cake)

Combine:

1 1/2 cups Butter Cream Frosting Mix (above)

1 Tbsp. water, plus one tsp. water

Stir until mixture is creamy (approx. one minute).

For a glaze, thin frosting by adding more water. Spread or drizzle over cake while it is still warm.

Chocolate Butter Cream Frosting
(for 9" layer cake)

Follow the recipe for Butter Cream Frosting (above). Add 2 Tablespoons cooking cocoa. Stir until mixture is creamy. Add 1/4 tsp. more water, if needed.

Orange Butter Cream Frosting
(for 9" layer cake)

Combine:
1 1/2 cup Butter Cream Frosting Mix (p. 90)
1 1/2 Tbsp. orange juice
1 Tbsp. grated orange peel
1/4 tsp. powdered lemon flavoring

Stir until mixture is creamy.

Banana Butter Cream Frosting
(for 9" layer cake)

Combine:
1 1/2 cups Butter Cream Frosting Mix (p. 90)
1/4 cup mashed banana
1/2 tsp. lemon juice

Stir until mixture is creamy.

Cream Cheese Frosting
(for 9" layer cake)

Soften and Stir:
2-4 oz. cream cheese
Add:
1 Tbsp. water, plus one tsp. water
1/4 tsp. powdered lemon flavoring
Add:
1-1 1/2 cups Butter Cream Frosting Mix (p. 90)

Stir until mixture is creamy.

Lemon Butter Cream Glaze

Combine:
1 cup Butter Cream Frosting Mix (p. 90)
1 1/2 Tbsp. water
2 tsp. lemon juice
1 tsp. lemon peel

Spread or drizzle over hot cake.

Sheet Cake
(Simply Scrumptious!)

Double the 9" Yellow Cake recipe (p. 85). Bake in a greased and floured cookie sheet or jelly roll pan. Prepare fruit sauce while cake is baking.

Combine in small sauce pan and cook until thickened:
1 1/2 cups water
1/4 cup concentrated lemon juice
1/4 cup sugar
3 Tbsp. cornstarch

Spread hot sauce over cake immediately after baking. After cake and sauce cool, top with alternate rows of sliced fresh or partially thawed frozen strawberries and peeled sliced kiwi. Serve with vanilla ice cream or whipped cream.

A Scandinavian favorite!

BROWNIE MIX

Combine:

5 cups sugar

3 1/3 cups flour

1 2/3 cups ground oatmeal (p. 70)

1 1/4 cups cooking cocoa

1/2 rounded cup dehydrated shortening or margarine

1/3 cup dehydrated egg white or whole egg

1 Tbsp. baking powder

1 1/4 tsp. salt

1/2 rounded tsp. cream of tartar

1/2 tsp. powdered vanilla

1/4 rounded tsp. baking soda

MINI-MIX

Combine:

1 cup sugar

2/3 cup flour

1/3 cup ground oatmeal (p. 70)

1/4 cup cocoa

2 Tbsp. dehydrated shortening or margarine

1 Tbsp. dehydrated egg white or whole egg

1/2 tsp. baking powder

1/4 tsp. salt

1/8 tsp. cream of tartar

1/16 tsp. powdered vanilla

1/16 tsp. baking soda

Brownies

Combine:
2 cups Brownie Mix (p. 93)
1/2 cup water
1/2 cup chopped walnuts

Bake at 350 degrees for 35 minutes in a greased and floured 8" x 8" pan. Cool slightly. Frost with Chocolate Butter Cream Frosting (p. 90).

Note: If dehydrated eggs are unavailable, make the mix without it using 2 cups Brownie Mix (p. 95), 2 beaten eggs, and 2 Tbsp. water. Bake as above.

Brownie Pudding

Spread Brownie batter (above) in an 8" x 8" pan.

Combine:
2 Tbsp. cocoa
1/3 cup sugar
1 1/2 cups hottest tap water

Dissolve cocoa and sugar in the water. Pour on top of the brownie batter. Bake at 350 degrees for 30 minutes. Serve hot or cold.

Fudge Sauce

1 cup Brownie Mix (p. 93)
1/4 tsp. powdered vanilla
1 cup hot water (add a little more if cooked sauce is too thick)

Bring mixture to a boil, stirring constantly, until thick and smooth.

WHOLE WHEAT BROWNIE MIX

Combine:
6 cups whole wheat flour
6 cups sugar
1 cup dehydrated margarine or butter
1 cup cooking cocoa
3/4 cup ground oatmeal (see p. 70)
1/3 cup whole egg
1 Tbsp. baking powder
1 tsp. baking soda
1/2 tsp. salt
1/2 tsp. powdered vanilla

MINI-MIX

Combine:
1 1/2 cups whole wheat flour
1 1/2 cups sugar
1/4 cup dehydrated margarine or butter
1/4 cup cooking cocoa
3 Tbsp. ground oatmeal (see p. 70)
1 1/2 Tbsp. whole egg
1 scant tsp. baking powder
1/4 tsp. baking soda
1/8 tsp. salt
1/8 tsp. powdered vanilla

Brownies
(A Whole Wheat Treat!)

Combine:
3 1/3 cups Whole Wheat Brownie Mix (above)
3/4 cup water
1/2 cup chopped walnuts

Spread in greased and floured 9" x 13" pan and bake at 350 degrees for 25 minutes. Cool slightly. Frost with Chocolate Butter Cream Frosting (p. 90).

95

BANANA BREAD MIX

Combine:

6 3/4 cups whole wheat or white flour
2 cups white sugar
2 cups brown sugar
2 1/4 cups dehydrated margarine or butter
1 cup powdered milk
1 cup dehydrated whole egg
3 Tbsp. baking powder
1 scant Tbsp. salt
1 scant Tbsp. baking soda
2 tsp. powdered vanilla
1 1/2 tsp. powdered butterscotch flavoring

MINI-MIX

Combine:

1 scant cup flour
1/3 cup white sugar
1/3 cup brown sugar
1/3 cup dehydrated margarine or butter
1 Tbsp. powdered milk
1 Tbsp. dehydrated whole egg
1 1/4 tsp. baking powder
1/2 tsp. salt
1/16 tsp. powdered vanilla
pinch of powdered butterscotch flavoring

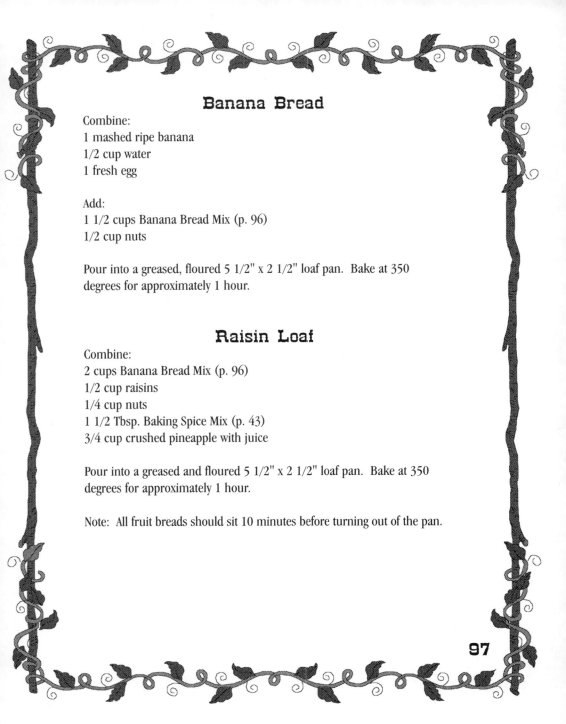

Banana Bread

Combine:
1 mashed ripe banana
1/2 cup water
1 fresh egg

Add:
1 1/2 cups Banana Bread Mix (p. 96)
1/2 cup nuts

Pour into a greased, floured 5 1/2" x 2 1/2" loaf pan. Bake at 350 degrees for approximately 1 hour.

Raisin Loaf

Combine:
2 cups Banana Bread Mix (p. 96)
1/2 cup raisins
1/4 cup nuts
1 1/2 Tbsp. Baking Spice Mix (p. 43)
3/4 cup crushed pineapple with juice

Pour into a greased and floured 5 1/2" x 2 1/2" loaf pan. Bake at 350 degrees for approximately 1 hour.

Note: All fruit breads should sit 10 minutes before turning out of the pan.

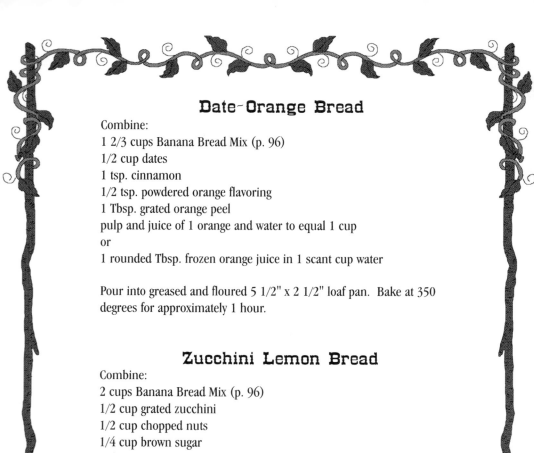

Date-Orange Bread

Combine:

1 2/3 cups Banana Bread Mix (p. 96)
1/2 cup dates
1 tsp. cinnamon
1/2 tsp. powdered orange flavoring
1 Tbsp. grated orange peel
pulp and juice of 1 orange and water to equal 1 cup
or
1 rounded Tbsp. frozen orange juice in 1 scant cup water

Pour into greased and floured 5 1/2" x 2 1/2" loaf pan. Bake at 350 degrees for approximately 1 hour.

Zucchini Lemon Bread

Combine:

2 cups Banana Bread Mix (p. 96)
1/2 cup grated zucchini
1/2 cup chopped nuts
1/4 cup brown sugar
1/4 cup, plus 2 Tbsp. water
1 Tbsp. grated lemon peel
1/2 tsp. powdered lemon flavoring
1 Tbsp. Baking Spice Mix (p. 43) or cinnamon

Pour into greased and floured 5 1/2" x 2 1/2" loaf pan. Bake at 350 degrees for approximately 1 hour.

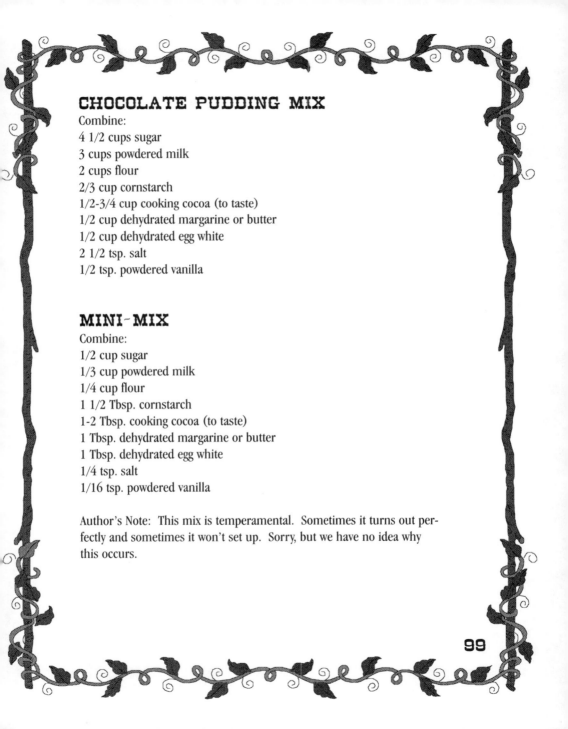

CHOCOLATE PUDDING MIX

Combine:
4 1/2 cups sugar
3 cups powdered milk
2 cups flour
2/3 cup cornstarch
1/2-3/4 cup cooking cocoa (to taste)
1/2 cup dehydrated margarine or butter
1/2 cup dehydrated egg white
2 1/2 tsp. salt
1/2 tsp. powdered vanilla

MINI-MIX

Combine:
1/2 cup sugar
1/3 cup powdered milk
1/4 cup flour
1 1/2 Tbsp. cornstarch
1-2 Tbsp. cooking cocoa (to taste)
1 Tbsp. dehydrated margarine or butter
1 Tbsp. dehydrated egg white
1/4 tsp. salt
1/16 tsp. powdered vanilla

Author's Note: This mix is temperamental. Sometimes it turns out perfectly and sometimes it won't set up. Sorry, but we have no idea why this occurs.

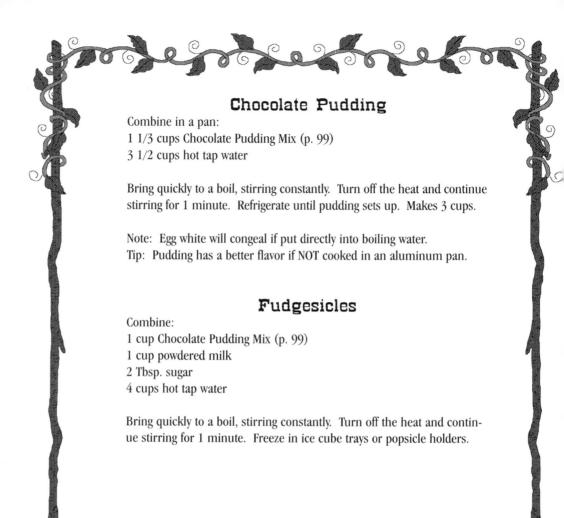

Chocolate Pudding

Combine in a pan:
1 1/3 cups Chocolate Pudding Mix (p. 99)
3 1/2 cups hot tap water

Bring quickly to a boil, stirring constantly. Turn off the heat and continue stirring for 1 minute. Refrigerate until pudding sets up. Makes 3 cups.

Note: Egg white will congeal if put directly into boiling water.
Tip: Pudding has a better flavor if NOT cooked in an aluminum pan.

Fudgesicles

Combine:
1 cup Chocolate Pudding Mix (p. 99)
1 cup powdered milk
2 Tbsp. sugar
4 cups hot tap water

Bring quickly to a boil, stirring constantly. Turn off the heat and continue stirring for 1 minute. Freeze in ice cube trays or popsicle holders.

HONEY CHOCOLATE CANDY MIX

Combine:

3 1/3 cups powdered milk

1/2 cup cooking cocoa (3/4 cup for dark chocolate lovers)

1 1/4 tsp. powdered vanilla

MINI-MIX

Combine:

1/3 cup powdered milk

2 Tbsp. cooking cocoa (3 Tbsp. for dark chocolate lovers)

1/8 tsp. powdered vanilla

Honey Chocolate Candy

Bring 1/2 cup honey to a boil and boil for 1 minute, 15 seconds. Remove from heat and add half cup Honey Chocolate Candy Mix (above). Blend with a wire whisk and let cool in the pan for 1-2 minutes. Pour candy onto a buttered pie plate or dish. Let it cool just long enough to be able to handle it. Butter your hands and, while candy is still warm, roll it to approximately the size of your little finger and coil it (not touching sides) on a buttered plate. For a soft candy (like a Tootsie Roll), cut into 1" pieces. Wrap individual pieces in waxed paper. For hard candy, cut into bite-sized pieces and dust with powdered sugar. Store in a covered candy dish.

HONEY BUTTERSCOTCH CANDY MIX
Combine:

3 1/3 cups powdered milk
1/2 cup dehydrated butter or margarine
1 tsp. powdered butterscotch flavoring

MINI-MIX
Combine:

1/3 cup powdered milk
2 Tbsp. dehydrated butter or margarine
1/8 tsp. powdered butterscotch flavoring

Honey Butterscotch Candy

Bring 1/2 cup honey to a boil and boil for 1 minute, 15 seconds.
Remove from heat and add 1/2 cup Butterscotch Candy Mix (above).
Add 1/2 cup chopped walnuts (optional). Blend with wire whisk and let
cool in the pan for 1-2 minutes. Pour candy onto a buttered pie plate or
dish. Let cool just long enough to be able to handle it. Butter your
hands and, while candy is still warm, roll to approximately the size of
your little finger and coil it (not touching sides) on a buttered plate. For
a soft candy, cut into 1" pieces and wrap in waxed paper. For hard
candy, cut into bite-sized pieces and dust with powdered sugar. Store in
covered candy dish.

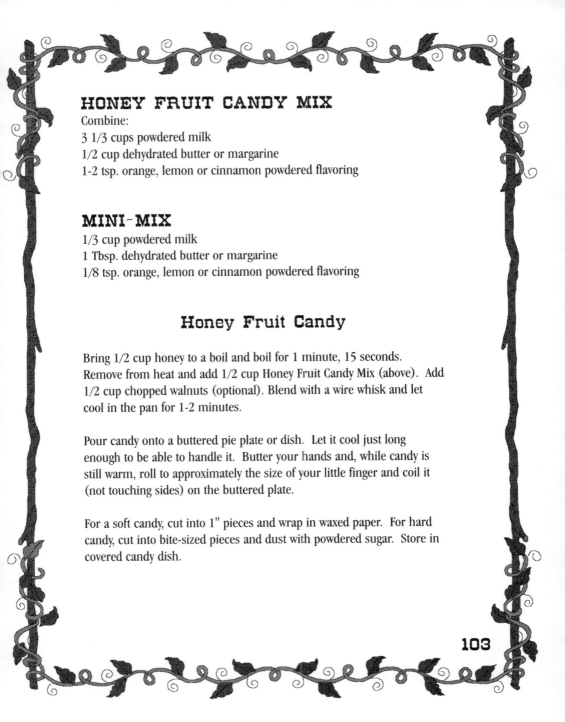

HONEY FRUIT CANDY MIX

Combine:

3 1/3 cups powdered milk
1/2 cup dehydrated butter or margarine
1-2 tsp. orange, lemon or cinnamon powdered flavoring

MINI-MIX

1/3 cup powdered milk
1 Tbsp. dehydrated butter or margarine
1/8 tsp. orange, lemon or cinnamon powdered flavoring

Honey Fruit Candy

Bring 1/2 cup honey to a boil and boil for 1 minute, 15 seconds. Remove from heat and add 1/2 cup Honey Fruit Candy Mix (above). Add 1/2 cup chopped walnuts (optional). Blend with a wire whisk and let cool in the pan for 1-2 minutes.

Pour candy onto a buttered pie plate or dish. Let it cool just long enough to be able to handle it. Butter your hands and, while candy is still warm, roll to approximately the size of your little finger and coil it (not touching sides) on the buttered plate.

For a soft candy, cut into 1" pieces and wrap in waxed paper. For hard candy, cut into bite-sized pieces and dust with powdered sugar. Store in covered candy dish.

ALPHABETICAL LISTING

Alfredo Delight . . . . .p. 57
Apple Bar Cookie Filling . . . . .p. 75
Apple Pancakes or Waffles . . . . .p. 37
Applesauce Spice Cake . . . . .p. 86
Au gratin Potatoes . . . . .p. 57
BAKING SPICE MIX . . . . .p. 43
BANANA BREAD MIX . . . . .p. 96
Banana Bread . . . . .p. 97
Banana Butter Cream Frosting .p. 91
Banana Pancakes or Waffles . . . . .p. 37
BARBECUE SAUCE MIX . . . . .p. 44
BAR COOKIE CRUST MIX . . . . .p. 74
Bar Cookie Fillings . . . . .p. 75
BASIC COOKIE MIX .p. 66
Bean Dip . . . . .p. 53
Beef Stroganoff . . . . .p. 59
BISCUIT MIX . . . . .p. 12
Braided Dinner Roll . . . . .p. 17
Braided Roll Fillings . . . . .p. 18
Bread, Homemade . . . . .p. 23
BREAD MAKER, Whole Wheat Bread . . . . .p. 24
Bread Sticks . . . . .p. 26
Breakfast Cake . . . . .p. 19
Broccoli Soup, Cream of . . . . .p. 60
BROWNIE MIX . . . . .p. 93
Brownie Pudding . . . . .p. 94
Brownies . . . . .p. 94
BROWNIES. WHOLE WHEAT MIX . . . . . .p. 95
Bundt Sweet Roll Bread . . . . .p. 27

BUTTER-CREAM FROSTING MIX . . . . . . p. 90
CAKE MIX, SUPERMARKET . . . . p. 84
Camping Ideas . . . . .p. 9
Caramel Honey Popcorn Cake . . . . .p. 83
Caramel Lite Sauce . . . . .p. 83
CARAMEL LITE MIX . . . . .p. 82
Caramel Pecan Muffins . . . . .p. 33
Caramel Popcorn . . . . .p. 82
Caramelized Onions . . . . .p. 35
CATALINA DRESSING MIX . . . . .p. 45
Cheddar Hamburger Supper . . . . .p. 61
CHEESE SAUCE MIX . . . . .p. 46
Cheesy Creamed Vegetables . . . . .p. 55
CHICKEN BAKING MIX . . . . .p. 20
Chicken Cream Puff Filling . . . . .p. 16
Chicken with Gravy . . . . .p. 41
Chicken or Tuna Filling . . . . .p. 18
Chili-Thick and Fast . . . . .p. 62
CHOCOLATE CHIP COOKIE MIX . . . . .p. 70
Chocolate Butter Cream Frosting . . . . .p. 90
Chocolate Fudge Cookies . . . . .p. 71
Chocolate Fudge Frosting .p. 88
CHOCOLATE PUDDING MIX . . . . .p. 99
Chocolate Pudding . . . . .p. 100
Christmas Fruit Cake . . . . .p. 79
Cinnamon Rolls . . . . .p. 27
Clam Chowder . . . . .p. 60
Cloverleaf Rolls . . . . .p. 26
Coleslaw . . . . .p. 63
Cornbread . . . . .p. 22
Cornbread, High-rise . . . . .p. 22
CORNBREAD MIX .p. 21
Cornbread Plus . . . . .p. 22
Country Gravy . . . . .p. 47

105

COUNTRY GRAVY MIX . . . . .p. 47
Crackers . . . . .p. 15
Cream Cheese Frosting .p. 91
Cream of Broccoli Soup .p. 60
Cream of Potato Soup . . . . .p. 60
Cream Puffs . . . . .p. 16
Creamed Vegetables . . . . .p. 55
Creamy Casseroles . . . . .p. 55
Crescent Rolls . . . . .p. 26
CRUMBLE TOPPING MIX . . . . .p. 69
Date Bar Cookie Filling .p. 75
Date-Orange Bread . . . . .p. 98
DEVILS FOOD WHOLE WHEAT CAKE MIX . . . .p. 89
Dip for Chips and Vegetables . . . . .p. 34
Drop Biscuits . . . . .p. 12
Enchiladas, Baked . . . . .p. 39
FRENCH DRESSING MIX . . . . .p. 48
French Onion Soup . . . . .p. 35
Fritters . . . . .p. 17
FROSTING MIX, BUTTER CREAM . . . . . . .p. 90
FROSTING MIX, COOKED . . . . .p. 88
Fruit Breakfast Pizza . . . . .p. 14
Fruitcake . . . . .p. 79
Fudge Sauce . . . . .p. 94
Fudgesicles . . . . .p. 100
German Chocolate Cake .p. 87
German Chocolate Frosting . . . . .p. 87
Gift Ideas . . . . .p. 8
GINGER SNAP COOKIE MIX . . . . .p. 68
Ginger Snap Cookies . . . . .p. 67, 68

GRAVY MIX, COUNTRY . . . . .p. 47

Homemade Bread . . . . .p. 23

HOMEMADE BREAD MIX . . . . .p. 23

Honey Butter . . . . .p. 22

HONEY BUTTERSCOTCH CANDY MIX . .p. 102

HONEY CHOCOLATE CANDY MIX . . . . . .p. 101

HONEY FRUIT CANDY MIX . . . . .p. 103

Honey Pancakes or Waffles . . . . .p. 37

Hot Chocolate . . . . .p. 71

HOT COCOA MIX . . . . .p. 71

HOT ROLL MIX . . . . .p. 25

House Dressing . . . . .p. 51

How to Make Mixes . . . . .p. 6

Important Tips . . . . .p. 7

INSTANT POTATO MIX . . . . .p. 30

ITALIAN SPICE MIX .p. 49

Italian Tomato Sauce . . . . .p. 52

Lasagna Supreme . . . . .p. 61

Lemon Butter Cream Glaze . . . . .p. 91

Lemon Cream Cheese Pie . . . . .p. 81

Maple Syrup . . . . .p. 38

MAPLE SYRUP MIX . . . . .p. 38

Marble Cake . . . . .p. 86

Mexican Dinner . . . . .p. 63

Mexican Pizza . . . . .p. 14

Mincemeat . . . . .p. 79

Mincemeat Bar Cookie Filling . . . . .p. 75

MUFFIN MIX . . . . .p. 32

Muffins . . . . .p. 32

Nacho Potato Bake . . . . .p. 62

OATMEAL COOKIE MIX (HONEY) . . . . .p. 76
OATMEAL COOKIE MIX (SUGAR) . . . . .p. 78
Oatmeal Honey Cookies . . . . .p. 77
Oatmeal Honey Cookies (Made with Sugar) . . . . .p. 78
Onion Rings . . . . .p. 37
ONION SOUP MIX . . . . .p. 34
Onion Steamed Rice . . . . .p. 34
Orange Butter Cream Frosting . . . . .p. 91
Orange Cake . . . . .p. 86
Orange Rolls, Heavenly . . . . .p. 27
ORIENTAL STIR FRY MIX . . . . .p. 64
Oven Baked Chicken . . . . .p. 20
PANCAKE AND WAFFLE MIX . . . . .p. 36
Pancakes or Waffles . . . . .p. 36
Pasta Perfect . . . . .p. 34
Patty-melt Filling . . . . .p. 18
Peanut Butter Cookies . . . . .p. 67
Picante' Nacho Sauce . . . . .p. 53
Picante' Sauce . . . . .p. 53
Pineapple Macaroons . . . . .p. 66
Pizza (Biscuit Crust) . . . . .p. 14
Pizza . . . . .p. 28
PLAY DOUGH MIX . . . . .p. 8
Pocket Bread . . . . .p. 28
Pocket Bread Fillings . . . . .p. 29
Popcorn Balls, Caramel Honey . . . . .p. 83
Pork & Beans Picnic . . . . .p. 18
POTATO COATING MIX . . . . .p. 31
POTATO MIX. INSTANT . . . . .p. 30
Potatoes, Oven Fried . . . . .p. 31
Potato Soup, Cream of . . . . .p. 60

Pot Pies . . . . .p. 13
Pumpkin Surprise . . . . .p. 33
Quiche — The Easy Way . . . . .p. 59
Raisin Loaf . . . . .p. 97
RANCH DRESSING MIX . . . . .p. 50
Rice, Onion Steamed . . . . .p. 34
Roast Beef Supreme . . . . .p. 35
Rolled Biscuits . . . . .p. 13
Rolls, Basic Dough . . . . .p. 25
SALAD DRESSING MIX . . . . .p. 51
Scalloped Potatoes . . . . .p. 58
Scones . . . . .p. 23
SEASONED SALT MIX . . . . .p. 43
Sheet Cake . . . . .p. 92
Shortcake or Sponge Cake .p. 85
Snickerdoodles . . . . .p. 73
Spaghetti Supper . . . . .p. 61
STIR FRY MIX, ORIENTAL . . . . .p. 64
Store Mixes, How To . . . . .p. 6
Stuffed Patties Supreme . . . . .p. 41
STUFFING MIX . . . . .p. 40
Stuffing, Quick and Easy . . . . .p. 40
Sugar Cookie Cutouts . . . . .p. 73
SUGAR COOKIE MIX . . . . .p. 72
SUPERMARKET CAKE MIX . . . . .p. 84
Swedish Oven Meatballs . . . . .p. 58
Swedish Rice Pudding . . . . .p. 81
SWEETENED CONDENSED MILK MIX . . . . .p. 80
Taco Filling . . . . .p. 18, 29
Taco Salad . . . . .p. 62
Tempura . . . . .p. 17
Thousand Island Dressing . . . . .p. 51

TOMATO SAUCE MIX . . . . .p. 52
TORTILLA MIX . . . . .p. 39
VEGGIE SALT MIX . . . . .p. 49
Waffles . . . . .p. 36
WHITE SAUCE MIX . . . . .p. 54
Yellow Cake . . . . .p. 85
Zucchini Lemon Bread . . . . .p. 98

Health Problems?

Need a low-salt diet?
Substitute equal amounts of powdered flavoring for salt in the mixes. The orange flavoring is wonderful in breads and rolls and the butter-scotch flavoring is great in cookies.

Problems with refined sugar?
Substitute fructose using only 1/3 to 1/2 as much sugar as is called for in the mixes.

Weight conscious?
Substitute equal amounts of applesauce for the oil in the recipes.

Wheat allergies?
Try using rice flour in the baking mixes. It works well for muffins and some cookies, but not for breads.

Notes

Notes

Notes

Notes

Notes

Notes

Notes

Notes

Notes

Notes

Notes

Notes

Mix-A-Meal Company
has a complete line of low-moisture
ingredients and flavorings for making
the fun and easy mixes in
Mix-A-Meal Cookbook

For more information please contact us at:
Mix-A-Meal Company
P.O. Box 971662
Orem, UT 84097-1662
phone 801-221-7465
fax 801-221-7449
info@mixameal.com
http://www.mixameal.com

MIX-A-MEAL COOKBOOK

Mixes & Recipes

Deanna Bean & Lorna Shute

Mix-A-Meal Company
Orem, Utah 84097-1662

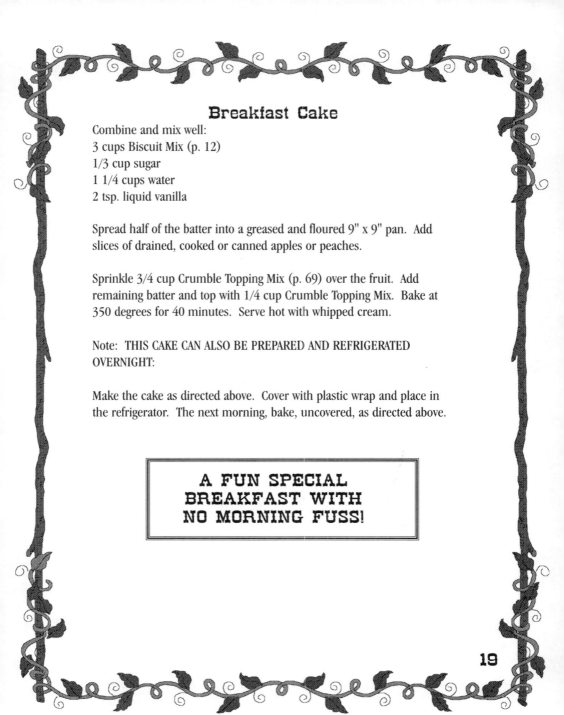

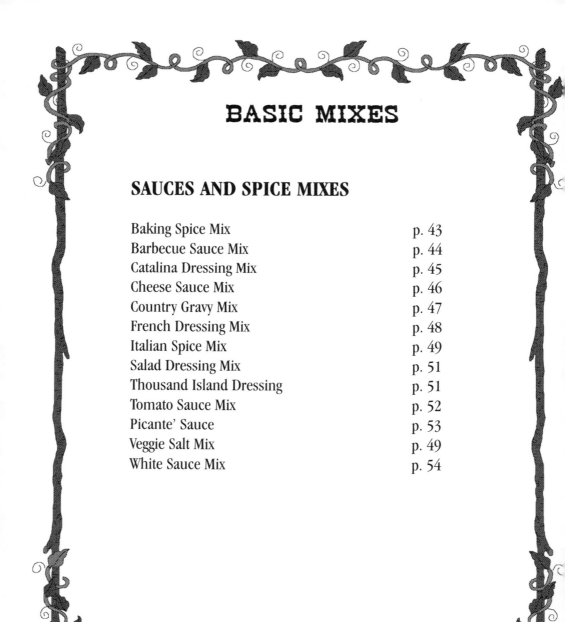

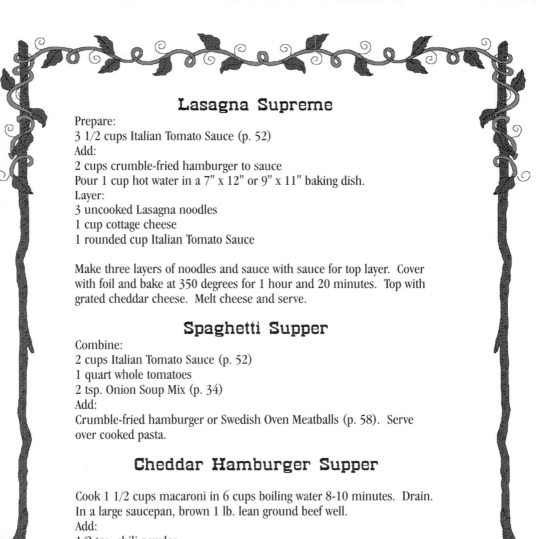